W9-BVN-461

MR. FOOD®

Cooks Like Mama

ALSO BY ART GINSBURG, MR. FOOD®

THE MR. FOOD® COOKBOOK

MR. FOOD®

Cooks Like Mama

but easier!

Art Ginsburg
MR. FOOD®

William Morrow and Company, Inc.
New York

ISBN 0-688-11127-0

Printed in the United States of America

BOOK DESIGN BY RICHARD ORIOLO

Dedicated to

Caryl, Carol, and Steve
Without whose caring and organization
I couldn't have written this book.

And to
Jennie—
That's My Mama!

Acknowledgments

Thanks to all the super public relations people who are an endless source of great ideas; to all the people who let me in on their Mamas' specialties and little family food "secrets"; and to my viewers who allow me into their homes every day. I sure hope I can return their welcome by adding some happiness to their days.

Thanks, also, to my editor, Maria Guarnaschelli, who knows how to guide and balance me with a smile, and to my agent, Bill Adler, who knows how to guide me with his foresight and practicality.

A special note of thanks to the food staff of the *Miami Herald*–Felicia, Linda, Linda, and Geoffrey–who, without knowing it, have helped keep my food sparks going for years. What a food section, up-to-the-minute and sensible!!

Special thanks to my "background team," Ethel, Chuck, Gersh, Tammy, and Flo, for their prodding, support, and patience during the many hours we put into creating this book. Also, thanks to the rest of my terrific staff in the MR. FOOD® organization whose team spirit keeps me going.

It takes a lot of people to do this right! I thank you all for sharing the OOH it's so GOOD!!™

The Gilroy Garlic Festival

The North Carolina Department of Agriculture

Keebler®

The Texas Department of Agriculture

Pace Foods

Durkee-French Foods, a division of Reckitt & Colman Inc.

The Noonday Onion Festival

Louis Kemp Seafood Co.
Louis Rich Co.
Oscar Mayer Foods Corp.
The American Dairy Association and Dairy Council
Thomas J. Lipton Co.
Delmarva Poultry Industry Inc.
Perdue Farms
The National Chicken Cooking Contest
Valley Grower Magazine
Lindsay Olive Growers
Sorrento Cheese Co.
The National Pork Producers Council
The New York Pork Council Women
International Apple Institute
Delta Pride Catfish Inc.
U.S.A. Rice Council
Hellmann's-Best Foods/CPC International
Cara Mia Artichokes
Hershey Foods Corporation
The California Turkey Industry Board
Sargento Cheese Co. Inc.
G & R Farms
The Belle Glade Corn Festival
The Florida Department of Agriculture
Borden, Inc., Product Publicity
The New York Cherry Growers Association
Western New York Apple Growers
Bisquick®, a registered trademark of General Mills, Inc.
Entenmann's
Mrs. Wilkes Boarding House, Savannah, Georgia
Grey Poupon
Sunkist Growers
SACO Foods Inc.

The California Date Administrative Committee

Lewis and Neale, Inc.

Miguel's Stowe Away

Italian Rose Garlic Products, Inc.

J. R. Brooks & Son, Inc.

The California Pistachio Commission

The Kansas Beef Council

Recipes courtesy of *Homemade Good News Magazine* and Savannah Foods & Industries, Inc., makers of Dixie Crystals Sugar: President's Chicken, One-Pot "Whatever," Country-Fried Steak, Noah's Squash, Pineapple Pudding, Pumpkin Squares, Summer Broiled Steak.

Recipes courtesy of McCormick®/Schilling®: Holiday Quick Bread, Strawberries Romanoff, and Strawberries Romanoff Cake.

Green Bean Bake recipe courtesy of Campbell's Soup.

Melted Provolone in Tomato Sauce recipe courtesy of Valerie Dominioni, *Great Italian Cooking* (New York: Doubleday, 1987).

Contents

Introduction

Our Mamas and Grandmas worked for hours to make the foods that we love to remember. They made everything from scratch—they had to. Mama shopped daily for fresh items, brought them home, and cut, chopped, boiled—you name it. Well, believe me, she wouldn't have done it that way if she hadn't had to! Today most of these things are already done for us by our food producers and markets. We buy items ready to use right off the shelf. Whether it's cake mixes, sauce mixes, pancake mixes, whatever, we should feel great about using them . . . 'cause **they're** great.

And what about time? It's the biggest consideration in modern cooking. We don't have time for intricate, gourmet recipes that require lots of steps and exotic ingredients, even if we wanted them. With all the outside activities of our two-income families, we need quick meals that we can make at home, so we can feel good about feeding our families homemade meals that are well balanced and reasonably priced yet still made to our own taste touches.

Today we have more mobility than Mama ever did. We shop in bigger markets with more fresh, processed, and convenience items to help us prepare our dinners "quick as a wink." Notice I said "prepare"—that's because that's really what we do with food today. We "prepare" more than we "cook." Well, sure! We usually stop in the market on the way home from some place and pick up something "ready to eat" or "ready to heat." Lots of times we make a salad along with it. We use canned and frozen foods—whatever is fast—and, presto, we have our meal.

Sometimes we're just too tired and we simply pick up take-out foods on our way home so that all we have to do is serve and eat.

Well, they're good, so why not? No, we don't do it all the time, but we do it a lot and it's OK.

There's still a lot of home preparation and cooking going on. Sometimes we cook on the weekend, making enough for a few meals. We do whatever we can, depending on our time and priorities. And, even with limited time we can *still* get some of Mama's tastes.

In fact, today it's easier to get those tastes. We've got more fresh herbs like the ones she used (but now they're available year 'round). We've got convenience items and mixes that take all the prelabor out of a recipe. Somebody else has done it for us. It's like having a helper in the kitchen doing a lot of the "rough part." We can buy salad veggies all cut and cleaned (and our produce is cleaner to start with). We've got some thick homestyle spaghetti sauces that are *almost* as good as Mama's (none will ever have her expert touch, but they come pretty close!). So, to relive the tastes that we remember, start with seasonings.

Ya know, there's no doubt that the spice rack is the most important tool in the kitchen. It's the world at our fingertips, our adventure, our joy, our nostalgia. And with everyone being more health-conscious today, we've all got to be more aware of what we're eating. We can usually do that and still get those old-fashioned tastes, too. What better way to start than with our spice rack?

We're constantly getting blasted with reports about nutrition and health-related food information. Now, I'm not a dietician or nutritionist, but I think you can enjoy the tastes you like if you're willing to fit recipes to your "special" situation. Nearly every recipe can be adapted for a particular restriction, whether it's low-fat, low-salt, low-sugar, whatever. Don't be afraid to try substitutions. For the most part, we can usually use yogurt for sour cream, ground turkey for beef, bacon bits or liquid smoke for bacon, etc. You know by now what you can and can't have, but be sure to check with your doctor if you have any questions.

Sometimes . . . no, most times, we'd like to make one special item that's simple, fast, inexpensive, exciting, and fun–something that'll be the talk of the table, a quick throw-together that can make the whole meal homemade. This book will help you do it; from a dip to dessert and everything in between, it's an "idea" book. There are no strict rules and regulations. You can usually use any brands and any substitutions. I've tried to suggest plenty of options, but be sure to include your own touches.

Half the fun is the experiment, and the success you enjoy when your experiment works. So, let this book be the "idea" that answers the number-one food question, "What should I make tonight?" Then, as I said, make it the book way, a modified-by-you way, or totally your very own way. It's a help even if it was just the "idea." It's the book that'll be at your fingertips on the kitchen counter, not on the never-used book rack or coffee table. They're all anybody-can-do-it-now recipes, recipes that smack of those old-time tastes without the old-time work.

Want recipes that take lots of ingredients or call for exotic, hard-to-get ingredients?

They're not here.

Want recipes that have a lot of preparation steps and keep you in the kitchen for hours (making your kitchen a total mess)?

They're not here.

Want recipes that you'll make once and never again?

They're not here, either.

BUT

If you want

- quick, easy, fun recipes that you can make with ingredients right off your kitchen shelf or the local supermarket shelf;
- recipes that'll make you a kitchen hero 'cause they taste like the ones Mama made, but without all the work and mess Mama had;
- recipes that let you use whatever brands you want and let you add your own touches;
- recipes that work even if you don't stick to hard rules and regulations;
- anyone-can-do recipes that can be put together in a snap—

then, BOY, OH BOY!! Have I got a book for you!!

Here it is! And you're gonna use it over and over again!!! And over and over again, you're gonna be saying

OOH it's so GOOD!!™

Fresh Herb Chart

If a recipe calls for fresh herbs and you want to use dried herbs instead, simply use half the amount of dried herbs. For instance, instead of using 1 tablespoon chopped fresh basil, use 1½ teaspoons dried basil. It works the same way with any type of herb. Whatever you choose, have fun!

Herb	Complementary Foods	Complementary Herbs
Basil	Tomatoes, tomato sauces, pasta, salads, fish, eggs, lamb, vegetables	Oregano, parsley, marjoram, thyme, mint, savory, chives
Chives	Carrots, cheese, eggs, fish, potatoes, green salads, soups, spinach, tomatoes	Basil, coriander, dill, marjoram, oregano, parsley, tarragon, thyme
Coriander (Cilantro)	Bread, cheese, chicken, eggs, fish, lamb, mushrooms, pork, green salads, soups, tomatoes	Chives, garlic, marjoram, oregano, parsley
Dill	Veal, chicken, fish, eggs, bread, potatoes, cucumbers, most vegetables, yogurt, sour cream, mustard	Tarragon, rosemary, marjoram, thyme, chives
Marjoram	Green beans, beef, cauliflower, eggplant, eggs, fish, mushrooms, soups, squash, stuffing, veal, poultry	Basil, bay leaf, chives, coriander, garlic, oregano, mint, parsley, rosemary, sage, savory, thyme

Fresh Herb Chart *(Continued)*

Herb	Complementary Foods	Complementary Herbs
Mint	Carrots, chicken, fruit, frosted beverages, lamb, salads, peas, potatoes	Basil, parsley, tarragon
Oregano	Beef, eggs, fish, lamb, pork, potatoes, salads, stews, tomatoes, veal, vegetables	Basil, bay leaf, chives, coriander, garlic, marjoram, mint, parsley, savory, thyme
Rosemary	Beef, bread, cauliflower, chicken, eggs, lamb, tomatoes, turkey, veal	Savory, thyme, sage
Sage	Dried beans, beef, bread, cheese, eggs, fish, soup, stuffing, turkey	Bay leaf, garlic, marjoram, oregano, parsley, rosemary, savory, thyme
Tarragon	Beef, eggs, fish, lamb, potatoes, salads, tomatoes, turkey, vegetables	Parsley, chives, bay leaf, dill, garlic, mint, savory
Thyme	Dried and green beans, beef, cheese, chicken, eggplant, eggs, fish, lamb	Basil, bay leaf, chives, garlic, marjoram, oregano, parsley, rosemary, sage, savory, tarragon

Compliments of Goodness Gardens

Seasoning Combinations

This can make it a little easier to get creative and adventurous (and playful)!

Poultry

Rosemary and thyme

Tarragon, marjoram, and onion & garlic powders

Cumin, bay leaf, and saffron or turmeric

Ginger, cinnamon, and allspice

Curry powder, thyme, and onion powder

Beef

Thyme, bay leaf, and instant minced onion

Ginger, dry mustard, and garlic powder

Dill, nutmeg, and allspice

Black pepper, bay leaf, and cloves

Chili powder, cinnamon, and oregano

Pork

Caraway seed, red pepper, and paprika

Thyme, dry mustard, and sage

Oregano and bay leaf

Anise, ginger, and sesame seed

Tarragon, bay leaf, and instant minced garlic

Fish and Seafood

Cumin and oregano

Tarragon, thyme, parsley flakes, and garlic powder

Thyme, fennel, saffron, and red pepper

Ginger, sesame seed, and white pepper

Coriander (cilantro), parsley flakes, cumin, and garlic powder

Potatoes

Dill, onion powder, and parsley flakes

Caraway seed and onion powder

Nutmeg and chives

Rice

Chili powder and cumin

Curry powder, ginger, and coriander (cilantro)

Cinnamon, cardamom, and cloves

Pasta

Basil, rosemary, and parsley flakes

Cumin, turmeric, and red pepper

Oregano and thyme

Vegetables

Green beans: marjoram and rosemary; caraway seed and dry mustard

Broccoli: ginger and garlic powder; sesame seed and nutmeg

Cabbage: celery seed and dill; curry powder and nutmeg

Carrots: cinnamon and nutmeg; ginger and onion powder

Corn: chili powder and cumin; dill and onion powder

Peas: anise and onion powder; rosemary and marjoram

Spinach: curry powder and ginger; nutmeg and garlic powder

Summer squash: mint and parsley flakes; tarragon and garlic powder

Winter squash: cinnamon and nutmeg; allspice and red pepper

Tomatoes: basil and rosemary; cinnamon and ginger

Fruits

Apples: cinnamon, allspice, and nutmeg; ginger and curry powder

Bananas: allspice and cinnamon; nutmeg and ginger

Peaches: coriander (cilantro) and mint; cinnamon and ginger

Oranges: cinnamon and cloves; poppy seed and onion powder

Pears: ginger and cardamom; black or red pepper and cinnamon

Cranberries: allspice and coriander (cilantro); cinnamon and dry mustard

Strawberries or Kiwi fruit: cinnamon and ginger; black pepper and nutmeg

Tips for Seasoning Low-Sodium Dishes

When eliminating salt:

Double the marinating time for poultry and meat for more complete flavor penetration;

Increase the amounts of spices and herbs in recipes by about 25 percent;

With long-cooking dishes, reserve about 25 percent of the seasonings to add during the last 10 minutes of cooking; herbs should be finely crushed.

NOTE: Black pepper may be routinely used in all dishes, including some fruits, as a basic seasoning. When listed in this chart, it's intended to be a major flavoring.

For best flavor results, keep spices in tightly covered containers, away from heat and light. Check them regularly. As soon as they lose their aroma and color they should be replaced.

Compliments of The American Spice Trade Association

Marinades for Beef, Chicken, Fish, and Pork

Amounts given are for 1 pound of any meat.
Combine 1/4 cup vegetable oil and 1 teaspoon Italian seasoning. Then for:

Steak or beef cubes, ADD	2 tablespoons red wine vinegar and 1½ teaspoons seasoned pepper
Boneless, skinless chicken breasts, ADD	2 tablespoons white wine vinegar and 1 teaspoon garlic salt (or 1¼ teaspoons garlic powder)
Lean fish, ADD	¼ cup white wine and 1½ teaspoons lemon and pepper seasoning salt (or 2 teaspoons lemon and pepper seasoning)
Pork chops (½ inch thick), ADD	¼ cup soy sauce and ½ teaspoon each of onion powder and ground ginger

Marinate for 20 to 30 minutes in the refrigerator, then broil or grill. From McCormick®/Schilling®

Equivalents and Substitutions

Mama never measured her ingredients. It was a pinch of this and a sprinkle of that. Well, I'm all for experimenting, but sometimes we need a place to start. And how about when we goof and think we've got something in the house but when we look for it . . . Oh, my gosh!! We're out!! Well, these equivalents and substitutions might be able to help us out of these jams. Just a glance will tell you what you can do.

Quick Measures

Dash	less than ⅛ teaspoon
3 teaspoons	1 tablespoon
4 tablespoons	¼ cup
5 tablespoons plus 1 teaspoon	⅓ cup
8 tablespoons	½ cup
10 tablespoons plus 2 teaspoons	⅔ cup
12 tablespoons	¾ cup
16 tablespoons	1 cup
2 tablespoons	1 fluid ounce
1 cup	½ pint or 8 fluid ounces
2 cups	1 pint or 16 fluid ounces
4 cups	2 pints or 1 quart or 32 fluid ounces
4 quarts	1 gallon or 64 fluid ounces
Juice of 1 lemon	about 3 tablespoons
Juice of 1 orange	about ½ cup
Grated peel of 1 lemon	about 1½ teaspoons
Grated peel of 1 orange	about 1 tablespoon

1 Pound* of	**Equals Approximately**
flour	4 cups
cornmeal	3 cups
sugar	2 cups
brown sugar	3 cups
confectioners' sugar	2½ cups
raisins	3 cups

1 Pound* of	Equals Approximately
rice	2 cups
macaroni	4 cups
meat	2 cups chopped
potatoes	2 cups diced or 2 large whole
cheese	4 cups grated

*One pound equals 16 ounces avoirdupois (our usual standard of weight measurement)

Substitutions

1 ounce chocolate	1 square or ¼ cup cocoa plus ½ tablespoon shortening
1 teaspoon baking powder	¼ teaspoon baking soda plus ½ teaspoon cream of tartar
1 tablespoon cornstarch	2 tablespoons flour (for thickening purposes)
1 cup milk	½ cup evaporated milk plus ½ cup water or 4 tablespoons powdered milk plus 1 cup water
1 tablespoon dehydrated minced onion	¼ cup finely minced fresh onion
1 teaspoon onion powder	⅓ of an onion
⅛ teaspoon garlic powder	1 garlic clove
1 tablespoon dehydrated parsley flakes	2 tablespoons fresh minced parsley

Special Note

As with many processed foods, package sizes may vary by brand. Generally, the sizes indicated in these recipes are average sizes. If you can't find the exact indicated package size, whatever package is closest in size will usually do the trick.

Appetizers

Appetizers and starters are the best! They set the tone for the rest of the meal.

Mama used to make some yummies to get us started off right. But today we don't have to make appetizers or starters that keep us busy in the kitchen all day. Nope!

We've got some quickies here that'll start us in the right direction to "yummy"—with a lot more fun and a lot less work. Start off with yummies, and everything after that is yummy, too. (And they're as easy as saying OOH it's so GOOD!!™)

San Antonio Wings

10 to 12 servings

W*ant something new and exciting for your entertaining that's different from what you had last week or the week before? Here's a wing recipe that's chicken light, Tex-Mex popular, and easy. And pardner, it's a new OOH it's so GOOD!!™*

- 5 pounds chicken wings (20 to 25)
- 1½ cups mild picante sauce
- 1½ cups ketchup
- 1 cup honey
- 1 teaspoon ground cumin

SAUCE

- 1 bottle (16 ounces) mild picante sauce
- 1 container (16 ounces) sour cream

Split the wings at each joint and discard tips; rinse, then pat dry. Place chicken wings in a shallow dish. In a bowl, combine 1½ cups picante sauce, ketchup, honey, and ground cumin; pour over chicken wings. Cover and marinate wings in refrigerator for at least 1 hour. Preheat oven to 350°F. Remove the wings from marinade and place on a cookie sheet; save marinade. Bake wings for 30 minutes. Brush wings with reserved marinade; turn and bake for 15 minutes more. Discard excess marinade. Preheat broiler and cook wings for 5 minutes more on each side. In a bowl, mix together sauce ingredients and serve as dipping sauce for wings.

NOTE: These wings are great served right from the oven *or* served cold or rewarmed on the grill at a picnic.

Cheese and Crab Dip

2 cups

Imagine how much attention you'll get when the barbecue gang sees you making this on the grill! You'll love making it for them to have along with crackers, tortilla chips, or chunks of fresh bread. And they'll be hanging around the grill waiting for it, so if you need some help, they'll be right there!

- 2½ cups (10 ounces) shredded Cheddar cheese
- 8 slices (one ounce each) American cheese (or 10 ¾-ounce slices)
- ⅓ cup milk
- 1 can (6½ ounces) crabmeat flakes, drained
- ½ cup dry white wine

In a heavy skillet, combine the cheeses and milk; place on the coolest part of the grill or over low heat on your stovetop and stir until the cheese melts. Stir in crabmeat and wine; cook until heated through.

NOTE: You can get the same great taste with imitation crabmeat (and it'll cost less, too!).

Sweet-and-Hot Dip

about 5 cups

This has so many uses! Try it with a fresh veggie platter . . . it's anything but the plain, old dip. For your cooked veggies, it's like a gourmet sauce. It even works wonders on fruit! I like to keep some on hand in the fridge in case friends drop over.

- 3 packages (8 ounces each) cream cheese, softened
- ½ cup orange marmalade
- ½ cup apricot jam or preserves
- ¼ cup hot pepper sauce
- ⅓ cup sour cream
- 3 tablespoons honey
- 1 tablespoon chopped fresh parsley
- 1 tablespoon lemon juice

In a bowl, combine all ingredients and mix thoroughly until smooth. Cover and refrigerate to "marry" the flavors.

Not-Fried Eggplant

30 to 35 pieces

Like eggplant but think it's a pain in the neck to make? Well, that may be true sometimes but not always. Here's how to make it easy and delicious!

- 1 medium to large eggplant
- 1 cup seasoned bread crumbs
- ⅓ cup grated Parmesan or Romano cheese
- ½ teaspoon salt
- ¼ teaspoon pepper
- 1 cup vegetable oil

Preheat oven to 375°F. Slice eggplant into ½-inch slices, then into 1-inch strips. In a bowl, combine bread crumbs, cheese, salt, and pepper. Place oil in a shallow dish; add eggplant strips and toss to coat. Then toss strips in bread crumb mixture and place on a foil-lined cookie sheet. Bake for about 20 minutes, then turn and bake for 5 minutes more, until golden brown.

NOTE: Serve with sour cream and chives, if desired.

Eggplant Appetizer

about 4 cups

Here's another great way to enjoy eggplant with no fuss and no muss! It's like an easy Sicilian-style caponata–such a rich-tasting relish.

- ½ cup olive oil
- 2 large onions, well chopped
- 3 large garlic cloves, minced
- 6 cups diced eggplant (about ¾ of a medium-sized eggplant)
- 1 can (14½ ounces) tomatoes, drained and chopped
- 2 tablespoons fresh lemon juice
- 1¼ teaspoons salt
- 1 teaspoon hot pepper sauce
- ¼ teaspoon pepper
- ¼ cup red or white wine vinegar
- 2 tablespoons sugar
- ¼ cup pitted black olives, chopped

Heat oil in a heavy saucepan. Add onion and cook for 3 minutes; add garlic and cook for 2 to 3 minutes more. Add eggplant and cook for at least 15 minutes more, stirring frequently, until eggplant is softened. Add tomatoes, lemon juice, salt, hot pepper sauce, and pepper. Simmer until mixture is soft and mushy, similar to relish. In a separate saucepan, heat vinegar and stir in sugar; add to eggplant mixture. Garnish with chopped olives.

NOTE: Serve cold or warm with crackers.

Shrimp Dip

about 2½ cups

They'll be saying "Olé!" when you serve this Tex-Mex–style dip. And we'll be saying "Olé!" 'cause it's so fast and easy!

- ½ pound cooked shrimp *or* 2 cans (4¼ ounces each) shrimp, rinsed and drained
- 1 small package (3 ounces) cream cheese, softened
- ⅓ cup Thousand Island dressing
- ⅓ cup mayonnaise
- ⅓ cup picante sauce
- 2 tablespoons grated or chopped onion
- 1 teaspoon horseradish

Finely chop the shrimp, reserving a few whole shrimp for garnish. In a large bowl, combine chopped shrimp with remaining ingredients; mix well. Spoon mixture into serving bowl, garnish with reserved shrimp, and chill.

NOTE: Serve with crackers, veggies, or tortilla chips and, for a change, try real or imitation crabmeat instead of shrimp. This also works well as a special salad dressing. Or try this: Spread on garlic bread, sprinkle with Parmesan cheese, and heat under the broiler for 5 minutes. Mmmm!!

Tex-Mex Dip

20 to 25 servings
(Yes, it feeds a mob!)

This is the perfect party dish. It looks so great and it gets everybody raving–even you, since you can make it a day ahead and enjoy it along with the rest of the gang. It's probably my favorite!

- 2 cans (9 ounces each) jalapeño bean dip
- 3 ripe avocados, mashed (about 1½ cups frozen mashed)
- ½ cup mayonnaise
- 1 tablespoon lemon juice
- 1 container (16 ounces) sour cream
- 1 package (1.25 ounces) taco seasoning mix
- 1½ cups (6 ounces) shredded Cheddar cheese
- 4 scallions, finely chopped
- 1 medium-sized tomato, diced

Spread bean dip on a large plastic or glass serving tray (about a 12-inch round). In a large bowl, combine avocados, mayonnaise, and lemon juice; spread over bean dip. In a separate bowl, combine sour cream and taco seasoning mix; spread over first two layers. Then sprinkle with cheese, then scallions, then tomato. Cover loosely and refrigerate overnight to "marry" the flavors.

NOTE: Just put this out with tortilla chips and stand back!

Cheesy Onion Puffs

12 servings

Wanna serve something that'll really be noticed by your party guests? This party hors d'oeuvre may look hard, but you'll know how homemade-easy it really is! (That's 'cause the ready-made frozen pastry sheets take all the work out of it.)

- 1 box (17¼ ounces) frozen puff pastry sheets, thawed (2 unbaked sheets)
- 1 container (15 ounces) ricotta cheese
- 2 cups (8 ounces) grated Cheddar cheese
- 1 medium-sized onion, finely chopped (about 2 cups)
- 2 eggs, slightly beaten
- ½ teaspoon salt
- 2 pinches cayenne pepper

Preheat oven to 375°F. Unfold 1 puff pastry sheet onto a 10″ × 15″ cookie sheet. In a large bowl, mix together the remaining ingredients, except the second pastry sheet. Spread cheese-onion mixture onto the unfolded pastry sheet. Unfold remaining puff pastry sheet and place over mixture. Bake for 40 to 45 minutes or until golden. Cool slightly, cut into squares, and serve warm.

NOTE: For even lighter puffs, you can use lowfat ricotta or Cheddar cheese. You can also cut down on the salt and add your favorite flavorings or fresh herbs.

Lobster Dip

about 2½ cups

For a lot of special and *delicious, try this great party dip that reminds us of summers at the seashore.*

- 8 ounces (½ pound) lobster meat, chopped
- 1 package (8 ounces) cream cheese
- ½ cup mayonnaise
- 1 teaspoon bottled minced garlic
- 1 teaspoon minced onion
- 1 teaspoon honey mustard

In a large bowl, combine all ingredients. Refrigerate until ready to serve.

NOTE: Serve with an assortment of crackers or cut-up veggies. You can substitute imitation crabmeat for the lobster meat if you want—it works well, too!

Texas Quick Dip

3½ cups

Drop-in visitors got you in a panic? No sweat! Here's a quick and easy dip they're sure to love. It just takes mixing four ingredients. (It sure tastes like more than that, though!)

- 2 packages (8 ounces each) cream cheese, softened
- ½ cup sour cream
- 1 jar (8 ounces) mild or medium salsa
- 1 teaspoon seasoned salt

In a medium-sized bowl, beat the cream cheese until smooth. Add sour cream. Fold in salsa and seasoned salt. Store in refrigerator but serve at room temperature.

NOTE: Serve with chips or veggies.

Danish Blue Cheese Spread

1¼ cups

Here's a surprisingly different taste that's holiday festive, too ('cause it's got little red and green pieces in it). With its great taste and great look I know you'll enjoy it doubly!

- 4 ounces cream cheese, softened
- ⅓ cup crumbled blue cheese, softened
- ¼ cup (½ stick) butter, softened
- ¼ cup ripe pimiento-stuffed olives, chopped
- 1 tablespoon chopped fresh parsley
- ¼ teaspoon garlic salt

In a large bowl, combine all ingredients and mix well, until smooth. Store in refrigerator but serve at room temperature.

NOTE: If you'd like a little smoother consistency, add a teaspoon or two of milk. There are lots of nice ways to serve this. You can place it in a serving bowl and surround it with your favorite crackers. Make a cheese ball this way: Line a medium-sized bowl with plastic wrap. Lightly press mixture into bowl, flattening top; cover with plastic wrap and refrigerate. When ready to serve, invert cheese ball onto platter, remove plastic wrap, and sprinkle with additional chopped parsley. Or you can toast it: Cut fresh French bread into ½- to ¾-inch slices. Spread generously with cheese spread. Broil 6 inches from heat for 4 to 5 minutes or until spread is bubbly.

French Pickled Mushrooms

6 servings

Sometimes we want to serve something that looks and tastes fancy but doesn't require a lot of fancy work. Well, here's one that'll do all those things. The nice relishy tang will really spark the tastebuds.

- 2 packages (12 ounces each) fresh mushrooms, stems trimmed
- ⅔ cup tarragon vinegar
- ½ cup vegetable oil
- 2 garlic cloves, crushed
- 1 tablespoon sugar
- 1½ teaspoons salt
- Dash fresh pepper
- 2 tablespoons water
- Dash hot pepper sauce
- 1 small onion, chopped
- 1 tablespoon chopped fresh parsley
- 1 tablespoon dried tarragon

In a large bowl, combine all ingredients, except mushrooms; mix well, then add mushrooms. Marinate overnight in the refrigerator, turning occasionally so that all of the mushrooms are soaked in the marinade. Store in a tightly covered container for up to 2 days.

NOTE: Instead of tarragon vinegar, you can use cider vinegar combined with an additional tablespoon of dried tarragon. This recipe will probably serve 8 to 10 people as a party hors d'oeuvre. Just serve with toothpicks and watch the mushrooms disappear!

Tarragon Dip

1 cup

H*aving the gang over? Here's a dip that's sure to be a hit—with you* and *with them! It's another "just-throw-it-together-fast" dip that we need when there's no time to fuss around.*

- 1 cup mayonnaise
- 2 teaspoons chopped onion
- 1 teaspoon dried tarragon
- 1 teaspoon chopped fresh parsley
- ½ teaspoon salt
- ½ teaspoon pepper

In a medium-sized bowl, mix together all ingredients. Store in refrigerator until ready to serve.

NOTE: This goes great with fresh veggies. If you want to add some zip, try it with a teaspoon of horseradish.

Really Italian Bread

24 to 30 servings

Stuck for an appetizer or a snack? How about something Italian-fancy and easy? (Probably the best upgraded garlic bread, too.)

- 1 1-pound loaf Italian bread, cut in half lengthwise
- 1 garlic clove, minced, or 1 teaspoon bottled garlic
- ⅓ cup olive oil
- ¼ teaspoon salt
- ¼ teaspoon pepper
- ½ cup thinly sliced scallions
- 1 small tomato, chopped
- 1½ cups (6 ounces) shredded mozzarella cheese

Preheat oven to 500°F. Place bread, cut-side up, on a foil-lined baking sheet; set aside. In a small bowl, mix together the garlic, olive oil, salt, and pepper; drizzle mixture over sliced bread. Sprinkle bread with scallions and tomato, then top with cheese. Bake in upper half of oven for 5 to 7 minutes or until cheese melts and edges of bread brown. Cut into 1-inch pieces and serve.

NOTE: You can garnish this with chopped sweet pepper or fresh herbs, if you like. Instead of a loaf of Italian bread, you can try this with a couple of submarine rolls if that's what you've got on hand. It'll be just as crunchy scrumptious!

Sweet-and-Sour Meatballs

about 60 small meatballs

One of my favorites! I think this tasty and easy recipe will be one of yours, too! Just be prepared to make it again and again, 'cause they'll be begging for more. This was one of the most looked-for items when I was in the catering business. (The rewarming the second day is the big secret to its being so rich.)

SAUCE

- 1 bottle (12 ounces) chili sauce
- ¼ cup ketchup
- ¼ cup currant or grape jelly
- 1½ cups firmly packed brown sugar
- 1 small onion, finely chopped
- 1 teaspoon lemon juice

MEATBALLS

- 1½ pounds ground beef
- ½ teaspoon salt
- 1 can (8 ounces) tomato sauce
- ½ cup dry bread crumbs

In a large saucepan or soup pot, combine all sauce ingredients and warm over medium-low heat. Meanwhile, in a large bowl, mix together all meatball ingredients; roll mixture into small meatballs. Add meatballs to sauce gradually and cook over medium heat for 35 to 40 minutes or until done, turning carefully from time to time so the meatballs don't break up. Refrigerate overnight to let flavors "marry"; skim off any fat that settles on top. When ready to serve, just rewarm.

NOTE: Just insert toothpicks . . . your company will do the rest!

Smoked Salmon Pâté

1 cup

W*ow–fancy pâté! Wow–an easy spread! That's really all that a pâté is, but you can impress your friends with this scrumptious appetizer–you don't have to tell them how easy it is to make.*

- ¾ cup chopped smoked salmon
- 1 small package (3 ounces) cream cheese (plain or with pimientos), softened
- ½ cup heavy cream
- 1 teaspoon lemon or lime juice
- 1½ teaspoons chopped fresh dill or ½ teaspoon dried dillweed
- Pinch of white pepper

In a large bowl, combine all ingredients. Using a hand mixer, blend with on and off strokes until mixture is workable and then blend on a low speed until mixture is well mixed and smooth. Store in refrigerator; serve at room temperature.

NOTE: You can add a small, seeded and finely chopped cucumber to the mixture for a slightly different taste. You can cover the pâté with chopped fresh parsley or pimiento; serve with rye or pumpernickel bread or your favorite crackers.

Spanish Cheese Tarts

12 servings

This can be Spanish, Portuguese, Central or South American, or Mexican–depending on the type of chorizo (sausage) used. The slight sweet of the crust makes it the perfect, easy "authentic."

- 2 packages (6 shells each) graham cracker tart shells
- 2 egg yolks, beaten
- 3/4 pound (12 ounces) sausage meat (chorizo, sage, scrapple, or cubed kielbasa)
- 1/4 cup minced onion
- 1 bottle (16 ounces) chunky salsa
- 2 eggs, beaten
- 3/4 cup (3 ounces) grated Monterey Jack cheese
- Dried oregano for sprinkling

Preheat oven to 350°F. Brush tart shells with beaten egg yolks and bake for about 3 minutes, until light golden. Remove from oven and let cool. Meanwhile, remove sausage from casing. Brown sausage and onion in a large skillet until sausage is well done and onion is tender. Spoon sausage mixture into cooled tart shells. Place salsa in a large bowl and add eggs; mix well. Pour the salsa mixture over the sausage mixture. Top each tart with cheese and sprinkle with oregano. Bake for 20 to 25 minutes, until cheese is melted and light golden.

NOTE: To make an Italian version, use Italian sausage and substitute spaghetti sauce for the salsa and shredded mozzarella for the Monterey Jack cheese. All other ingredients are the same. You can also use minced turkey sausage or your own favorite kind–the flavor will still be delicious!

Chicken Puffs

8 servings

Don't know what to do with that leftover chicken? How about a simple chicken sensation? They'll never know it's from leftovers–honest! In fact, I've been buying chicken just to make these. They can be a main course, also; simply serve two or three of them. They're a really fancy-looking and -tasting guaranteed "rave"!

- 2 small packages (3 ounces each) cream cheese, softened
- 5 tablespoons butter or margarine, melted and divided
- 2 cups diced cooked chicken
- 1/4 cup milk
- 1/2 teaspoon pepper
- 2 tablespoons minced onion
- 2 tablespoons diced pimientos
- 2 cans (8 ounces each) crescent rolls

Preheat oven to 350°F. In a large bowl, mix together the cream cheese and 3 tablespoons melted butter. Add the chicken, milk, pepper, minced onion, and pimientos; mix well. Separate each package of crescent rolls into four rectangles. Divide the chicken filling evenly and spoon into center of each rectangle. Bring ends up together and pinch closed. Brush with remaining 2 tablespoons of melted butter. Place puffs on a greased cookie sheet and bake for 12 to 15 minutes or until golden brown.

NOTE: If you'd like, sprinkle puffs with a touch of your favorite spice. You can use all white-meat chicken, all dark, or a combination–whatever you have on hand or prefer.

Easy Seafood Dip

about 3 cups

Here's a dip I make at holiday time that's so amazingly quick and simple. You can serve it anytime, though, 'cause it makes any gathering holiday special!

- 1 container (8 ounces) sour cream
- 1 cup chopped cooked shrimp or crabmeat
- ⅓ cup finely chopped green pepper
- ⅓ cup finely chopped onion
- ⅓ cup finely chopped celery
- ⅓ cup bottled chili sauce
- 1 tablespoon horseradish
- 1 tablespoon fresh lemon juice

In a large bowl, combine all ingredients; chill. Keep refrigerated until ready to serve.

NOTE: Serve with vegetable and bread dippers. Imitation crabmeat or shrimp work well, too.

Parmesan Pita Triangles

about 20 servings

Pita is practically perfect! With pita bread on hand you'll always be able to make a quick appetizer. Try this quick garlicky bread appetizer that can be even better topped with chili, salsa, chicken salad, or whatever you choose!

- 5 pita bread rounds
- 6 tablespoons (3 ounces) melted butter
- Garlic powder for sprinkling
- Grated Parmesan cheese for sprinkling

Preheat oven to broil. Cut each pita into 6 pie slice-shaped wedges. Separate each wedge into 2 triangles and place on cookie sheets. Brush each pita triangle with melted butter. Sprinkle garlic powder and Parmesan cheese over each triangle and broil for 1 to 2 minutes, until cheese is bubbly and lightly browned. Serve warm.

Relishes and Sauces

A relish is so much . . .
It's

something savored
something that tweaks the tastebuds
something that'll be the sharp point of each bite
something that'll be the extra touch on the table

Relishes and sauces are those extra special "somethings" that raise the level of whatever they're served under, over, or with. Mama spent hours making them from great bargain in-season items. Today we can throw them together in no time. With the markets full of goodies to help us, we can make relishes and sauces that still do the same things they always did. For instance, roast beef done just right is wonderful, but serve it with gourmet-sounding but simple-to-make Carpaccio Sauce or Garlic Sauce . . . WOW!! Get the picture?? Here are some easy ones. Go ahead, look like a hero!

Really Shortcut "Béarnaise" Sauce

2 cups

W*anna "dress up" a piece of meat without going to a lot of trouble? Here's how all the Mamas in France do it today. (They don't like a lot of work either!)*

- 1 envelope (1.25 ounces) Hollandaise sauce mix
- ¼ cup mayonnaise
- ¼ cup sour cream
- 1 teaspoon dry white wine
- 1 teaspoon dried tarragon
- 1 teaspoon Worcestershire sauce
- 1 teaspoon salt (or to taste)

In a saucepan, prepare Hollandaise sauce according to package directions. Mix in remaining ingredients. Transfer to serving bowl and refrigerate until ready to use. Serve at room temperature.

Fresh Bell Pepper–Celery Chowchow

4½ cups

Sometimes one little homemade item on the table makes the whole meal taste homemade. Here's a Pennsylvania Dutch–type relish that everybody'll love. They'll say you shouldn't have fussed–and you didn't!

- 4 cups coarsely chopped celery
- 1 cup coarsely chopped green bell pepper
- 1 cup coarsely chopped red bell pepper
- ½ cup coarsely chopped onion
- ½ cup wine vinegar
- 1 tablespoon mixed pickling spice
- ⅓ cup sugar
- 1 tablespoon salt
- 1 teaspoon caraway seed

Place celery, green and red bell pepper, and onion in a large bowl; set aside. In a saucepan, combine vinegar and pickling spice; bring mixture to a boil and boil for 5 minutes. Strain mixture, then add sugar, salt, and caraway seed; pour over vegetables. Cover and refrigerate for 24 hours before serving. Store in refrigerator for up to 1 week.

NOTE: This is a great accompaniment to any meal. It can even take the place of a salad.

Middle Eastern Meat Sauce

6 servings

How about something different for a change? Like meat sauce without tomatoes–that's right, no tomatoes! This one is a Middle Eastern version and it's so simple to prepare. And there are loads of other exciting ways to prepare meat sauce. Just by changing a few ingredients, you can visit a different country every time you serve it!

- 1½ pounds lean ground beef
- 1 large onion, finely chopped
- 2 garlic cloves, minced
- 1 teaspoon dried mint
- 1 teaspoon chopped fresh parsley
- ¼ teaspoon dried oregano
- ¼ teaspoon ground cinnamon
- Salt to taste
- Pepper to taste
- 1 container (8 ounces) yogurt or sour cream
- 2 teaspoons lemon juice

In a large skillet, brown the ground meat with the onion and garlic; pour off excess fat. Stir in the mint, parsley, oregano, cinnamon, salt, and pepper, then the yogurt and lemon juice. Over a medium heat, simmer, covered, for 20 minutes to allow flavors to blend.

NOTE: If the sauce is too thick, you can thin it with some broth or water. Serve over rice or pasta and sprinkle ¼ cup chopped fresh parsley and paprika over the top as a garnish. If you'd like to make it Italian style, add some crushed fennel seed and skip the cinnamon.

Easy Gravy

***H**omemade gravy is one of our favorite "home comfort" treats. We can have it in minutes anytime we've got this easy mix on hand. And be bold–try a different variation every time.*

Gravy Mix

about 1¾ cups dry mix

- 1 jar (2¼ ounces) chicken or beef flavor instant bouillon (about ½ cup)
- 1½ cups all-purpose flour
- ½ teaspoon pepper

In a medium-sized storage container or plastic bag, combine all ingredients. Store, tightly covered, at room temperature. Shake or stir before using to make Gravy (see below).

NOTE: For interesting flavor variations add any of the following to the gravy mix: Italian: 1 teaspoon Italian seasoning and ½ teaspoon garlic powder; French: 1½ teaspoons dried tarragon; Southwest: 1½ teaspoons chili powder, ½ teaspoon cumin, and ¼ teaspoon garlic powder.

Gravy

about 1¾ cups

- 3 tablespoons margarine
- ¼ cup Gravy Mix (see above)
- 1¾ cups water or milk

In a medium-sized skillet or saucepan, melt the margarine. Stir Gravy Mix into margarine; cook and stir until golden brown. Add water, then cook and stir until thickened and all the bouillon is dissolved.

NOTE: Serve with meat, poultry, or mashed potatoes.

Spanish Sauce

about 4 cups

Turn an everyday meal into one so homemade special they'll think it's a holiday! It sure works for Spanish adventure . . . you'll see. (And it's basically a bottled spaghetti sauce.)

- 2 tablespoons olive oil
- 1 small onion, chopped
- 2 celery stalks, chopped
- 1 green bell pepper, chopped
- 2 garlic cloves, chopped
- 2 tablespoons chopped fresh parsley
- 1 bottle (28 to 32 ounces) prepared spaghetti sauce

In a saucepan, heat olive oil until moderately hot; sauté onion, celery, bell pepper, and garlic until golden. Add parsley and spaghetti sauce to vegetable mixture and heat through.

NOTE: Serve over pasta. I sometimes like to use a chunky spaghetti sauce and bottled garlic and parsley instead of fresh (it's quicker!). I also add a little "heat" (in the form of hot sauces) to spice it up—anything works!

Garlic Sauce

1½ cups

Here's a prize-winning recipe that'll make you a winner every time you use it. That's because anything it's served with becomes steps above regular!

- 5 to 6 garlic cloves, peeled
- 2 egg *yolks*
- 3 tablespoons fresh lemon juice
- 1 tablespoon prepared mustard
- ½ teaspoon salt
- 1 cup olive oil
- ½ cup fresh basil leaves

In a blender jar, place garlic, egg yolks, lemon juice, mustard, and salt; cover and blend until smooth. With blender running, very slowly pour in olive oil in a thin stream. Turn off blender, add basil, and blend briefly until basil is coarsely chopped.

NOTE: Serve over roasted or grilled meat, chicken, or fish, and cooked or raw vegetables. I especially like it over summer tomatoes, cucumbers, and sweet onions. As with any dish containing raw eggs, be sure to store the sauce in the refrigerator until ready to use. If you have any concern over using a recipe containing raw eggs, then skip this one.

My Own Barbecue Sauce

about 1⅓ cups

***W**ant a barbecue taste that's quick and easy without having to start up the grill? No problem!*

- 1 cup ketchup
- ¼ cup firmly packed brown sugar
- 2 tablespoons white vinegar
- 1 tablespoon instant minced onion
- 2 tablespoons Worcestershire or steak sauce
- 1 teaspoon dry or 2 tablespoons prepared mustard

In a medium-sized bowl, mix together all ingredients. Store in refrigerator until ready to use. Stir before using.

NOTE: This is best when used for roasting or grilling chicken.

Carpaccio Sauce

2 cups

This fancy-sounding, simple-to-make sauce goes great with any meat. When you serve your roast beef with a dollop of this it'll be like Mama put her special taste stamp on it. This is another recipe from my catering days. When I served it with roast beef . . . WOW!!

- 2 cups mayonnaise
- 4 anchovy fillets
- 2 teaspoons capers
- 2 bunches fresh parsley, coarsely chopped
- 4 teaspoons red wine vinegar
- 1/4 teaspoon salt
- 1/4 teaspoon pepper

Combine all ingredients in a blender jar; blend until very smooth. Store in refrigerator.

NOTE: If serving sauce over warm meat, allow sauce to reach room temperature before using.

Baked Cranberry Sauce

about 2½ cups

Once you see how easy and delicious this sauce is, cranberries won't be just for Thanksgiving anymore!

- 4 cups cranberries (one 12-ounce bag is about 3 cups)
- 2 cups sugar
- ¼ cup water

Preheat oven to 350°F. In a 9″ × 13″ glass baking dish, stir together the cranberries, sugar, and water. Cover dish with foil and cook for 50 to 60 minutes, stirring occasionally, until cranberries pop. Refrigerate until ready to use.

Dill Sauce

2 cups

***H**ave any leftover meat, fish, or chicken? Wanna do something a little different with it? Well, cut it into chunks and serve it with this sauce, and they'll think you started from scratch! And we know how well dill goes with lots of things . . . so it's a sure winner.*

- 1 envelope (1.25 ounces) Hollandaise sauce mix
- ¼ cup mayonnaise
- ¼ cup sour cream
- 1 teaspoon dried dillweed
- 1 teaspoon Worcestershire sauce
- ⅛ teaspoon salt (or to taste)

In a saucepan, prepare Hollandaise sauce according to package directions. Mix in remaining ingredients. Transfer to serving bowl and refrigerate until ready to use.

NOTE: This sauce is also great served with chunked vegetables.

Cheesy Dill Sauce

3 cups

Here's dill again!! Make everyday fish or steak into something special—and it's so easy to do! There's plenty of room for playing with extra or different spices, too.

- 2½ cups mayonnaise
- ¾ cup sour cream
- Juice of 1 lime or lemon
- 3 tablespoons snipped fresh dill
- 2 teaspoons pepper
- 1 garlic clove, mashed
- ¼ cup grated Parmesan cheese
- 1 teaspoon Dijon mustard
- ¼ cup finely minced onion

Place all ingredients in a large bowl and mix. Store in refrigerator until ready to use.

NOTE: If you add 2 tablespoons milk, this will make a great salad dressing. For a little different taste, try adding 1 teaspoon sweet pickle relish.

Portuguese Sauce

about 2½ cups

Here's a way to make a plain ol' piece of meat, chicken, or fish come alive with the exotic flavors of Portugal. When the sauce is mixed with a little imagination, you can travel to a faraway place, without leaving your dinner table. I've been using this a lot lately!

- 3 tablespoons olive oil
- 1 large onion, chopped
- 1 can (28 ounces) whole peeled tomatoes, drained
- 3 garlic cloves, chopped
- 1 bay leaf
- 1 teaspoon dried thyme
- ½ teaspoon crushed red pepper
- ½ teaspoon sugar
- ½ cup chopped black olives
- ¼ cup chopped fresh parsley

In a large skillet, heat olive oil; sauté onion over medium heat just until softened. Add tomatoes, garlic, bay leaf, thyme, red pepper, and sugar. Reduce heat and simmer for 30 minutes, stirring occasionally. Stir in olives and parsley and cook for 10 minutes more. *Remove bay leaf before serving.*

NOTE: Serve with steak, fish, or chicken.

Old-Time Hot Dog Sauce

10 servings

Remember those great Fourth of July celebrations when you were a kid? With hot dogs from the barbecue that were topped with just the right sauce? Well, we can have a summer full of new tastes from this old Coney Island–type favorite!

- ½ pound ground beef
- 1 medium-sized onion, chopped
- 1 can (8 ounces) tomato sauce
- 1 tablespoon chili powder
- ½ teaspoon Worcestershire sauce

In a large skillet, sauté ground beef and onion over medium heat, stirring often, until beef is browned. Add tomato sauce, chili powder, and Worcestershire sauce. Bring mixture to a boil, lower heat, and simmer for 10 minutes, stirring occasionally.

NOTE: For a real taste treat, place cooked hot dogs on rolls and top with sauce; you should have enough for about 10. Add your favorite regular toppings, too. To make the sauce taste as if it came from a New York pushcart, add a little cinnamon. Oregano will give it a Greek or Italian flavor and a teaspoon of ground cumin will make it an authentic chili dog.

Soups and Chowders

Nothing says "Mama" more than soup. Remember those bowls full of that good stuff that tasted better and better the closer we got to the bottom of the bowl?

Whether it was the soup so thick you could eat it with a fork, or that thin, clear soup dotted with fresh greens, we could use it as a filler or make it into a whole meal. (Those are the two schools of soup lovers, you know—the "thicks" and the "thins"!)

Sure, a large bowl of soup, some crusty bread to dunk in it, a salad, maybe a chunk of cheese . . . it's a whole meal (and so down-home easy!). The down-home part is so adaptable, too, 'cause by simply adding things like Mama did we can change the whole character of the soup.

For instance, a shake of oregano and fennel seed will give your soup an Italian sausage flavor. With a bay leaf and caraway seed, it's German. With a couple tablespoons of soy sauce and a shake of ginger . . . Oriental.

If your base soup doesn't call for carrots and you've got extras, go ahead! They'll give it your own touch. Who knows? It might be better than the original. See what I mean?? Inexpensive, warming, welcoming, delicious soup. It's Mama's tastes all over again—but so much easier today . . . you'll see.

So, experiment, play, enjoy! You'll surely bring back that satisfied feeling.

Creole Fish Chowder

4 servings

Here's a no-fuss way to serve up a cozy meal at the end of a busy work day—and it's all in one pot. And the best part about it is everyone will think you fussed! With some crusty bread and a salad?? WOW!!

- ½ cup chopped onion
- ¼ teaspoon cayenne pepper
- 2 cans (8 ounces each) tomato sauce
- ½ teaspoon garlic powder
- 2 bay leaves
- 1 can (28 ounces) whole tomatoes
- 1 bag (16 ounces) frozen mixed vegetables
- 1 pound frozen fish fillets, thawed slightly and chunked

In a soup pot, combine the onion, cayenne pepper, tomato sauce, garlic powder, bay leaves, and whole tomatoes; simmer for 10 minutes. Add frozen vegetables and simmer for 10 minutes more. Add fish; cover and simmer for another 8 to 10 minutes or until fish flakes with a fork. *Be sure to remove bay leaves before serving.*

NOTE: If you want, you can use fresh fish instead of frozen. Or for a change, you can use canned stewed tomatoes and add your favorite seasonings to spice it up. It's so easy!

Coastline Chowder

8 servings

Here's the "anything goes" way they make chowder along the coast. No fancy rules and regulations, just throw in whatever fish you have on hand–and serve up a hearty chowder rich enough to be the whole meal!

- 5 cups water
- 1 can (14½ ounces) tomatoes, whole or crushed
- 1 can (8 ounces) tomato paste
- 1 cup dry white wine
- 1 medium-sized onion, chopped
- 1 carrot, chopped
- 1 celery stalk, chopped
- ¼ cup coarsely chopped fresh parsley
- 2 garlic cloves, minced
- 2 bay leaves
- 2 teaspoons salt
- Pepper to taste
- Dash hot pepper sauce (optional)
- 2 pounds fresh or frozen fish fillets or a combination of fillets and seafood, thawed

In a soup pot, combine all ingredients, *except* fish; bring to a boil. Lower heat and cook, uncovered, for 20 to 30 minutes, until vegetables are tender. Cut fish into large chunks; add to pot and bring just to boiling. Reduce heat and simmer, covered, for 8 to 10 minutes more or until fish flakes with a fork. *Before serving, remove bay leaves and discard.*

NOTE: Serve with fresh, crusty bread and butter or sharp cheese.

Southwestern Chowder

10 to 12 servings

Easy, easy, easy!! But will they like it? You can bet on it . . . it's like stacking the deck so everybody wins.

- 2 tablespoons vegetable oil
- ½ pound smoked turkey or turkey ham, cubed
- 1 to 2 large onions, chopped
- 6 cups (about 2½ pounds) potatoes, peeled and cubed
- 2 quarts water
- 2½ cups (about 5 6-ounce cans) tomato paste
- 2 cups mild picante sauce
- 1 package (12 ounces) American cheese, cubed

In a soup pot, combine oil, turkey, and onions; cook until onions are soft. Add potatoes, water, tomato paste, and picante sauce. Bring mixture to a boil, reduce heat, and simmer, covered, for about 20 to 30 minutes or until potatoes are tender. Stir in cheese and simmer until cheese melts completely. Serve immediately.

Zesty Tomato Soup

4 to 5 servings

Tomato soup won't be dull and ordinary once we add these special touches. Why, it'll be fancy enough to serve to company! (But make it even when it's just the family, 'cause they're special, too!)

- 1/4 cup (1/2 stick) butter
- 1/2 cup chopped onion
- 1/2 cup chopped green bell pepper
- 1/4 cup all-purpose flour
- 2 teaspoons instant beef bouillon
- 1/8 teaspoon salt
- 1/8 teaspoon pepper
- 2 1/2 cups milk
- 1 can (14 1/2 ounces) stewed tomatoes, puréed

In a soup pot, melt the butter; sauté onion and green pepper until tender, about 5 minutes. Add flour, bouillon, salt, and pepper and stir until smooth. Remove from heat and gradually stir in milk. Heat to boiling, stirring constantly, for about 1 minute. Stir in puréed tomatoes and heat to serving temperature.

NOTE: Serve with your favorite sandwich. To make the soup homier, you can add cooked rice and get Tomato Rice Soup. You can also add cooked broccoli or green beans and call it Garden Tomato Soup.

Shortcut Potato Soup

6 to 8 servings

This tastes like Mama's old-fashioned potato soup, except that I add potato flakes to thicken it even more–in less time. (And, like Mama's, it's even better the second day!)

- 1½ cups diced onion
- ¼ cup (½ stick) butter or margarine
- 4 cups large-diced potatoes (about 2 to 2½ pounds)
- 1 carrot, coarsely grated
- 2 cups water
- 1 teaspoon salt
- ½ teaspoon pepper
- 1 teaspoon dried dillweed
- 3 cups milk
- 2 tablespoons chopped fresh parsley
- ¼ cup potato flakes

In a large saucepan, brown the onion in the butter. Add the potatoes, carrot, water, salt, pepper, and dillweed. Cook on low until potatoes are creamy, about 45 minutes. Stir in the milk and parsley and continue cooking until mixture is heated through. Stir in the potato flakes.

NOTE: If you'd like, add frozen peas or broccoli at the milk stage.

Mexican Bean Soup

6 to 8 servings

From coast to coast, everybody loves the taste of Mexico. And most everybody loves soup! Well, here's an easy one that you can enjoy without even nearing the border.

- ½ pound ground beef
- 1 medium-sized onion, chopped
- 1 can (14½ ounces) whole tomatoes, chopped
- 1 can (15 ounces) red kidney beans
- 1 can (7 to 8 ounces) kernel corn
- 1 can (8 ounces) tomato sauce
- 2 teaspoons chili powder
- 1½ cups water
- Crushed tortilla chips for topping (optional)

In a large saucepan, brown beef with onion. Stir in remaining ingredients and simmer for about 30 minutes. Serve topped with crushed tortilla chips.

NOTE: I sometimes add ½ teaspoon cumin and a few shakes of hot pepper sauce to "heat it up."

Easy Mushroom Barley Soup

8 to 10 servings

On a cold winter night, there's nothing better than a hearty bowl of soup. With a salad and some bread, it's a whole meal! And when it's everybody's Mama's thick, rich mushroom soup there's really nothing better. Here's her basic one, but she used to throw a lot of extras in, depending on what leftovers needed a home.

- 4 large onions, chopped
- 6 large carrots, peeled and sliced
- 1 pound mushrooms, thinly sliced
- 1 pound stew beef, cut into small cubes
- 8 cups beef broth (made from a soup base or a mix)
- 1 cup medium barley
- ½ teaspoon salt
- ½ teaspoon pepper

Place all ingredients in a soup pot and bring to a boil, stirring occasionally. Reduce heat and simmer, partially covered, for about 1 hour.

NOTE: If you'd like, add 1 or 2 shots of Irish whiskey with the other ingredients for added flavor. It'll make it really Irish! In addition to the base recipe ingredients, you might want to add some cut-up hot dogs and a teaspoon of caraway seed for German-style soup. Or you can even add ½ teaspoon each of oregano and rosemary for Italian-style soup.

Bean Chili

about 12 cups

Here's a favorite chili recipe of mine that gets more raves and cheers than there are beans in the pot. This is another one that makes a whole meal when served with a salad–but it makes a great chili chowder side dish, too!

- 2 tablespoons olive oil
- 1 large onion, chopped
- 1 cup picante sauce
- 1 cup chicken broth
- 2 cans (28 ounces each) crushed tomatoes (or whole tomatoes, chopped)
- 1 can (15 ounces) pinto beans, drained
- 1 can (15 ounces) red kidney beans, drained
- 1 can (15 ounces) black-eyed peas, drained
- 1 teaspoon cumin

In a large saucepan or Dutch oven, heat the olive oil; add onion and sauté until softened. Add remaining ingredients, bring to a boil, then reduce heat and simmer for 10 minutes.

NOTE: Add some browned meat or sausage and it's a straight, fast chili. I sometimes use a little salt or garlic to give it a "tang." If you have a favorite combination of beans, they'll work fine, too.

Chinese Soups

Everybody thinks there's something mysterious about making those wonderful soups we get in Chinese restaurants. Well, they're just good old-fashioned chicken soup. Of course, if you really want the secret to the Chinese soup mystery . . . it's what they put in afterward that makes the difference! Well, take a look.

Egg Drop Soup

4 servings

3½ cups water
1 envelope (2.25 ounces) chicken noodle soup mix
1 egg, beaten

In a medium-sized saucepan, bring the water to a boil; stir in soup mix. Reduce heat and simmer for 5 to 10 minutes. With a fork, quickly stir in the egg, a little at a time, until it congeals. Serve.

Shortcut Won Ton Soup

4 servings

- 4 cups water
- 1 envelope (2.25 ounces) chicken noodle soup mix
- ½ cup frozen peas
- ½ cup sliced celery
- ¼ pound ham, cut into thin strips
- Sliced scallion for garnish

In a large saucepan, combine the water, soup mix, peas, and celery. Bring to a boil, then lower heat and simmer for 5 minutes. Add ham and stir. Serve topped with scallion.

NOTE: If you add crisp noodles just before serving, it will be like the soup you love in Chinese restaurants. You can also use cooked chicken or turkey instead of ham. You might even add some precooked meat ravioli during the last few minutes of cooking. Then it'll be similar to the Chinese won ton.

Meatball Soup

4 servings

Remember Mama's meatball soup? Back in the '50s? And how everybody loved it? And how easy it was to make? With a few shortcuts, we can make it even easier and better than before. Yippee!

MEATBALLS

- ½ pound ground beef
- ¼ cup uncooked long-grain rice
- 1 egg, beaten
- ⅛ teaspoon pepper

SOUP

- 3½ cups water
- 1 envelope (1.1 ounces) beefy onion soup mix
- ¼ teaspoon dried thyme

In a large bowl, combine meatball ingredients. Shape mixture into 1-inch meatballs and place on a cookie sheet or waxed paper; set aside. In a saucepan, combine soup ingredients; bring to a boil. Carefully drop meatballs into boiling soup; reduce heat and simmer, covered, for 25 minutes.

NOTE: I sometimes like to use ground turkey or chicken for a lighter change. You can also add cut-up fresh or frozen veggies if you like (whatever ones are left over from last night's supper will work just great).

Scandinavian Cabbage Soup

6 to 8 servings

It may sound exotic, but it tastes delicious and it's so easy to prepare. You'll feel great serving this treat to your family and they'll feel great 'cause they'll think you really fussed! (Only you'll know the truth!) Oh, and talk about reasonable!!

- ½ cup (1 stick) margarine
- 2 cups chopped cabbage
- 1 cup sliced onion
- 1 cup sliced celery
- 1 cup frozen peas, thawed
- 1 cup thin carrot slices
- 1 can (16 ounces) cream-style corn
- 3 cups milk
- 1 teaspoon salt
- ¼ teaspoon pepper
- 1 teaspoon dried thyme
- ¼ teaspoon garlic powder
- 2 cups (8 ounces) shredded Cheddar cheese

In a large soup pot, melt the margarine; sauté the cabbage, onion, celery, peas, and carrots until tender, about 8 to 10 minutes. Add the corn, milk, salt, pepper, thyme, and garlic powder; simmer for about 15 minutes. Add the cheese, stirring until melted, and serve.

South-of-the-Border Party Soup

4 to 6 servings

H*ow about a throw-together Tex-Mex soup that'll turn your party into a homemade fiesta¿¿*

- 1 tablespoon butter or margarine
- ½ cup diced red bell pepper
- ½ cup diced green bell pepper
- 2 cans (10¾ ounces each) condensed cream of potato soup
- 10¾ ounces milk (1 soup can)
- ½ cup picante sauce
- ½ teaspoon ground cumin
- ¾ cup (3 ounces) shredded Monterey Jack cheese
- ¾ cup (3 ounces) shredded Cheddar cheese
- Chopped fresh parsley (optional)

In a large saucepan, heat the butter until moderately hot; cook red and green peppers until tender, about 5 minutes. Add soup, milk, picante sauce, and cumin, stirring until smooth. Heat mixture until hot, stirring occasionally (do not boil). Add cheeses, stirring until melted. Ladle into soup bowls and sprinkle with parsley, if desired.

NOTE: Serve with additional picante sauce.

Easy Blueberry Soup

5 to 6 servings

Ever try the chilled blueberry soup the gourmet restaurants serve? Well, they think it's brand new, but Mama made it for years with leftover berries. Sure, she knew how easy it is, also.

- 3 cups plus 2 tablespoons water
- 1 quart fresh blueberries, stemmed, rinsed, and drained
- 1 cup sugar
- 2 tablespoons cornstarch
- Sour cream or yogurt for topping

In a large saucepan, bring the 3 cups water to a boil. Add the blueberries and sugar, stirring just until sugar is dissolved; set aside. In a small bowl, mix together the cornstarch and remaining 2 tablespoons water to make a paste. Add cornstarch mixture to saucepan and return blueberry mixture to a boil. Let cool, then cover and refrigerate. Serve well chilled with a dollop of sour cream or yogurt.

NOTE: For an extra special tang add a squeeze of fresh lemon or lime juice when boiling the blueberries, water, and sugar.

Tropical Fruit Soup

about 4 servings

Cold fruit soup—we'd like to make it but we think it's too much bother. Well, the good news is it's as easy as can be, especially the no-cook ones like this one. So, enjoy! Imagine . . . no cooking!

- 3/4 cup canned pineapple chunks, drained (1 8-ounce can)
- 1 small banana
- 1 cup pear, peach, or apricot fruit juice nectar, chilled
- 1/2 cup half-and-half, chilled
- Kiwi slices for garnish

In a blender jar, combine the pineapple chunks and banana; purée. Add the nectar and half-and-half and blend just until mixed. Chill thoroughly before serving. Garnish with kiwi slices.

Chilled Strawberry Soup

about 4 servings

Want a great way to use those beautiful fresh strawberries? Wanna be the envy of all your friends? Well, just make this easy, delicious soup and you'll accomplish both!

- 2 cups crushed fresh strawberries
- ½ cup sugar
- ¾ cup ginger ale

In a large bowl, mix together all ingredients. Refrigerate. Serve chilled. (Now, can it be any easier than that??)

Chicken and Turkey

There's no question that poultry has grown to be one of our most popular choices today. And why not? Not only are so many people now into "light" foods, but it's also become one of our best values.

When Mama and Grandma made it, it was something of a luxury . . . "a chicken in the pot every Sunday." Well, today it's less expensive than ever. With our new growing and transportation methods, we can always buy chicken in a variety of ways—from whole to just our favorite parts. It's readily available and usually on sale in some form or other for even better value. Ditto for turkey. So, it's no longer just a holiday-time treat.

It's always a treat 'cause it fits our lifestyle so perfectly: It's versatile and fast, too. There's always some quick way we can make chicken or turkey (depending on what parts we use or how it's cut, of course)—in the oven, on top of the stove, or on the grill.

No matter who we make it for, sometimes all it takes to please them is a little "sprinkle of this" or a "shake of that." We can have Mama-style chicken and turkey that's healthier and easier than ever. Go ahead, make it whole, in parts, in sandwiches, casseroles, or whatever . . . but make it soon 'cause they'll love it!

Timetable for Roasting Chicken at 350°F.

Parts	Approximate Weight	Final Meat Thermometer Reading (in degrees F.)	Approximate Cooking Time* (in minutes)
Whole (unstuffed)	3½ lbs.	185 to 190	1 hr. 15 min.
(stuffed)	3½ lbs.	185 to 190	1 hr. 40 min.
(cut-up)†	3½ lbs.	180	50 to 60
4 Thighs	4½ to 6½ oz. each	180	45 to 50
4 Thighs (boneless)	3½ to 5½ oz. each	160	30 to 35
4 Breast Halves	8 to 10 oz. each	180	50 to 55
4 Breast Halves (boneless)	5 to 7 oz. each	160	30 to 35
4 Drumsticks	3½ to 5½ oz. each	180	45 to 50
4 Leg-Thigh combinations	8½ to 10½ oz. each	185 to 190	50 to 55
4 Quarters (2 breasts, 2 leg-thighs)	12 to 14 oz. each	185 to 190	60 to 65

*Cooking times are based on chicken taken directly from the refrigerator.

†Approximate weight of pieces of a cut-up 3½-lb. broiler-fryer chicken:

Thighs	5 to 6 oz. each
Drumsticks	3½ to 4 oz. each
Breasts with rib (halves)	9 to 10 oz. each
Wings	3 to 4 oz. each
Whole back	8 to 9 oz. each

Courtesy of the National Broiler Council

Timetable for Roasting a Whole Turkey

As simple as 1—2—3!

Turkey is one of today's best meat buys, both nutritionally and economically. Whole turkeys are sold oven-ready: dressed, washed, inspected, and packaged. After turkeys leave the processing plant, no hands touch them until time for kitchen preparation.

It takes only 6 minutes to prepare a defrosted whole turkey for roasting (without stuffing).

If stuffing is desired, it's often best prepared separately, placed in a covered casserole, and cooked with the turkey during the last hour of roasting time.

Follow label instructions for roasting, or use these simple directions to obtain a beautiful golden brown, ready-to-carve-and-eat turkey:

1. Thawing: (If turkey is not frozen, begin with step 2.) *Do not thaw poultry at room temperature.* Leave turkey in original packaging and use one of the following methods:

No hurry: Place wrapped turkey on tray in refrigerator for 3 to 4 days; allow 5 hours per pound of turkey to completely thaw.

Fastest: Place wrapped turkey in sink and cover with cold water. Allow about ½ hour per pound of turkey to completely thaw. Change water frequently.

Refrigerate or cook turkey when it is thawed. Refreezing uncooked turkey is not recommended.

Commercially frozen stuffed turkeys should *not* be thawed before roasting.

2. Preparation for roasting: All equipment and materials used for storage, preparation, and serving of poultry must be clean. Wash hands thoroughly with hot soapy water before and after handling raw poultry. Use hard plastic or acrylic cutting boards to prepare poultry.

Remove plastic wrapping from thawed turkey. Remove giblets and neck from the body and neck cavities. To remove neck, it may be necessary to release legs from band of skin or wire hock lock. Rinse turkey inside and out with cool water, pat dry with a paper towel, and return legs to hock lock or band of skin; or tie together loosely. Tuck tips of wings under back of turkey. Neck skin should be skewered with a poultry pin or round toothpick to back of turkey to provide a nice appearance for serving at table. The turkey is now completely ready for roasting.

3. Open pan roasting: Place turkey breast-side up on flat rack in shallow roasting pan, about 2 inches deep. Insert meat thermometer deep into thickest part of thigh next to body, not touching bone.

Brush turkey skin with vegetable oil to prevent drying. Turkey is done when meat thermometer registers 180 to 185°F. and drumstick is soft and moves easily at joint.

Once skin of turkey is golden brown, shield breast loosely with rectangular-shaped piece of lightweight foil to prevent over-browning.

Roasting at 325°F.

Approximate Weight (in pounds)	**Approximate Cooking Time* (in hours)**
6 to 8	2¼ to 3¼
8 to 12	3 to 4
12 to 16	3½ to 4½
16 to 20	4 to 5
20 to 24	4½ to 5½

*Approximate Roasting Time: Factors affecting roasting times are type of oven, oven temperature, and degree of thawing. Begin checking turkey for doneness about one hour before end of recommended roasting time.

Courtesy of the California Turkey Industry Board

Very Ritzy Italian Chicken

4 to 6 servings

It's so fancy you won't believe how easy it is! The best part of this one is that you can make it (and clean it up!) ahead of time. That leaves plenty of time to enjoy all the applause! And no, it's not low in calories, but it sure is right for that special time or special person.

- 3 whole chicken breasts, split, skinned, and boned
- 2 eggs, slightly beaten
- 1 cup seasoned bread crumbs
- 3 tablespoons olive oil
- 6 slices mozzarella cheese
- 1 pint heavy cream
- 1 cup grated Parmesan cheese
- 2 tablespoons chopped fresh parsley
- Salt to taste
- Pepper to taste

Preheat oven to 350°F. Dip the chicken breasts in the eggs. Place the bread crumbs in a shallow bowl; coat the chicken with the bread crumbs. In a large skillet, heat the oil until moderately hot. Place the chicken in the frying pan and brown lightly on both sides. Remove from pan and place in a baking dish. Top each breast with a slice of mozzarella cheese. In a saucepan, mix together the heavy cream, Parmesan cheese, parsley, salt, and pepper. Cook until mixture is hot and has thickened. Pour over chicken and bake for 25 minutes or until cheese is melted and light golden.

NOTE: This is great served over pasta. Sometimes I get the whole dish together and put it aside in the refrigerator for a day or two. Then, 30 minutes before I'm ready to serve it, I bake it. Sometimes I'll sprinkle a little nutmeg or paprika on top for a little different taste.

President's Chicken

4 servings

You can't beat these flavor combinations. The taste will make all *your company feel special (and wait 'til you tell them what it's called!).*

SAUCE

- ¼ cup (½ stick) butter or margarine
- Juice of 1 lemon
- ¾ teaspoon salt
- ½ teaspoon paprika
- ½ teaspoon dried oregano
- ¼ teaspoon garlic powder
- ¼ teaspoon pepper

- 4 whole chicken breasts, skinned and boned

Preheat oven to broil. In a large skillet, mix together sauce ingredients; cook over low heat until butter has melted. Place chicken breasts in a shallow baking dish; pour sauce over the chicken. Broil for 30 to 35 minutes or until done, turning chicken occasionally to coat well with sauce.

NOTE: Serve over rice or noodles and drizzle with the pan drippings for a delicious flavor boost. You can use chicken breasts with the bone in and even leave the skin on but, if you do, remember to cook them a little longer.

Olympics Chicken

4 servings

This unusual dish was a contest winner named for the Seoul Olympics. It's got rich, full Korean flavors in every bite. With Oriental flavors being so popular, it's really a winner–and so easy, too!

- 2 tablespoons vegetable oil
- 8 chicken thighs, skinned
- 10 garlic cloves, coarsely chopped
- 1 teaspoon crushed red pepper
- ¼ cup white vinegar
- 3 tablespoons soy sauce
- 2 tablespoons honey
- ¼ teaspoon ground ginger

In a large skillet, heat the oil until moderately hot. Add the chicken and cook until brown on all sides, about 10 minutes. Add garlic and red pepper to chicken; cook for 2 to 3 minutes, stirring occasionally. Drain off excess fat. In a small bowl, mix together the vinegar, soy sauce, honey, and ginger; add to the chicken. Reduce heat and simmer, covered, for 15 to 20 minutes or until chicken is fork-tender and fully cooked.

NOTE: Serve with rice. When cooked, the garlic becomes mellow and is not overpowering. However, if you prefer, you can start with 2 garlic cloves and ¼ teaspoon red pepper. Adapt it to your own taste!

Crunchy Chicken

4 servings

Chicken breasts sautéed with a nut coating may sound trendy but once you taste this one, you'll want to keep it around as one of your Southern home-cooking standards. Heck! We were making it this way before pecans became so "in"!

- 1 cup pecans, finely ground
- ½ cup grated Parmesan cheese
- ½ teaspoon garlic salt
- ½ teaspoon dried basil
- Lemon juice for dipping
- 2 whole chicken breasts, split, skinned, boned, and flattened
- 2 tablespoons olive oil

In a large shallow dish, combine pecans, cheese, garlic salt, and basil. Place lemon juice in another shallow dish; dip chicken in juice, then coat with pecan mixture. In a large nonstick skillet, heat oil until moderately hot. Add the chicken; cook for 3 to 5 minutes on each side or until golden and cooked through.

NOTE: Sometimes I like to use turkey, veal, or pork cutlets instead of chicken. (Remember to flatten them!) For different flavors I try different nuts and sometimes I add a little pepper to make the dish spicier. I even use lime juice instead of lemon for variety.

My Own Sausage Burgers

(or . . . My Own Turkey Sausage)

4 to 6 patties

Yes, ground turkey is usually somewhat bland, but not if it's seasoned well. So, how about using it to make your own Italian sausage burgers? That ought to make them sit up and take notice! And the lean of the ground turkey mixed with these seasonings is everything we want today.

- 1 pound ground turkey
- 1 small onion, chopped
- 1 egg, beaten
- 2 tablespoons bread crumbs
- 1 teaspoon dried thyme
- 1 teaspoon salt
- 1 teaspoon fennel seed, crushed
- ½ teaspoon garlic powder
- ½ teaspoon black pepper
- ¼ teaspoon cayenne pepper

In a large bowl, mix together all ingredients. Form mixture into patties and broil, grill, or pan-fry in vegetable oil until meat is done and no longer pink.

Cheesy Chicken

4 servings

There really couldn't be an easier way to make such great-tasting chicken. It only takes 3 ingredients—that's right, three! Easy enough?

- ¼ cup (½ stick) butter or margarine, melted
- 2 whole chicken breasts, split (skinned, if desired)
- 3 cups cheese crackers, crushed

Preheat oven to 350°F. Place melted butter in a shallow dish; roll chicken breasts in butter, then in cracker crumbs. Arrange chicken pieces in a baking dish. Bake for 50 to 60 minutes, until chicken is fork tender and fully cooked.

NOTE: To cook in the microwave, prepare as above. Cover the baking dish with waxed paper and microwave on high for 12 to 15 minutes. Rotate dish ½ turn after the first 6 or 7 minutes. Let stand, covered, for 2 to 3 minutes before serving. Please remember that cooking time may vary slightly depending on the wattage of your microwave. When you use the microwave try putting the dish under the broiler for a few minutes to brown the chicken up a bit; then it's really "cooked."

"Remember" Chicken

4 to 6 servings

These tastes and aromas will surely take you back to the days when Mama spent all day in the kitchen. This chicken is truly, truly that memorable.

- 1 3- to 4-pound chicken, cut into 8 pieces
- Flour as needed (seasoned with a little salt, pepper, and paprika)
- 3 tablespoons butter
- 3 tablespoons vegetable oil
- ½ cup chopped onion
- 2 cans (15½ ounces each) black-eyed peas
- ½ cup chicken broth
- ½ teaspoon dried oregano
- 1 medium tomato, chopped

Rinse chicken, pat dry with paper towels, and coat with seasoned flour. In a Dutch oven, heat butter and oil; add chicken and cook slowly, until golden brown on both sides. Remove chicken and keep warm. Sauté onion in the Dutch oven until tender, about 5 minutes. Add black-eyed peas, chicken broth, and oregano; bring to a boil. Arrange chicken over the black-eyed pea mixture, pressing the chicken into the peas. Sprinkle tomato over the top; reduce heat and simmer, covered, for 35 to 40 minutes or until chicken is fork-tender and fully cooked.

NOTE: For a different taste, try water or wine instead of the chicken broth. You can also use any canned beans—great Northern, cannellini, limas, etc.—whichever is on hand or on sale. And, instead of oregano, why not try tarragon or thyme? There are so many options with this dish and they're all delicious!

Mustard-Topped Turkey Cutlets

2 to 3 servings

I *guarantee this'll be a treat you'll want to repeat and repeat. The reason?? Easy turkey and plenty of easy seasonings. (The Pilgrims never had it so good!!)*

- 4 to 5 turkey breast cutlets (about 1 pound)
- 2 teaspoons vegetable or olive oil
- ¼ cup mayonnaise
- 3 tablespoons seasoned bread crumbs
- 2 tablespoons dry white wine
- 1 tablespoon prepared mustard
- ¼ teaspoon sugar

Preheat oven to broil. Brush turkey cutlets with the oil on both sides. In a small bowl, combine mayonnaise, bread crumbs, wine, mustard, and sugar; set aside. Place turkey on broiling pan; broil 6 inches from heat source for about 3 minutes on each side, until done and no pink remains. Spread mustard mixture over turkey; broil for 1½ to 2 minutes more or until topping is hot and golden brown.

Chicken Hash

8 to 10 servings

This is so good with leftover chicken or turkey that you'll probably want to make it even when there are no leftovers. That's OK, because it's great with store-bought, precooked chicken or turkey, too!

- ¼ cup (½ stick) butter or margarine
- 3 cups diced onions
- 3 cups diced red and/or green bell pepper
- 5 cups diced cooked chicken or turkey (about 1¾ to 2 pounds)
- 4 cups peeled, diced cooked potatoes (about 2 to 2½ pounds)
- 1 can (10¾ ounces) cream of celery soup
- ¼ teaspoon salt
- ¼ teaspoon black pepper
- 1 egg, beaten
- ⅓ cup grated Parmesan cheese

Preheat oven to 400°F. In a Dutch oven, melt the butter; add onions and sauté until tender, about 5 minutes on medium-high heat. Add the red and/or green peppers, chicken, potatoes, soup, salt, and pepper; cook, stirring occasionally, until mixture is heated through, about 10 minutes. Coat a 9"x13" baking dish with nonstick vegetable spray; spoon in chicken mixture. Brush egg over top of mixture, then sprinkle with Parmesan cheese. Bake for 10 to 15 minutes or until golden.

Nice-Crust Chicken

6 servings

This one's a nice crunchy change from regular roasted chicken 'cause the crust is like the "treat" part.

- 3 whole chicken breasts, split and skinned
- 1/4 cup prepared mustard
- 1 cup bread crumbs
- 1/4 cup grated Parmesan cheese
- 1 tablespoon dried minced onion
- 3/4 teaspoon salt
- 1/4 teaspoon garlic powder
- 1/4 teaspoon dried oregano
- 2 to 3 tablespoons butter or margarine, melted
- 6 tablespoons sour cream or plain low-fat yogurt

Preheat oven to 350°F. Brush the chicken breasts with mustard; set aside. In a large shallow dish, mix together the bread crumbs, Parmesan cheese, onion, salt, garlic powder, and oregano. Roll the chicken in the bread crumb mixture to coat. Place chicken in a large, lightly greased baking pan, meaty side up. Drizzle chicken with melted butter. Bake, uncovered, for 50 minutes or until fork-tender. Arrange chicken on a serving dish and top with sour cream or yogurt.

Southwest Chicken

6 to 8 servings

W*hether you need something fancy or homey, these campfire flavors can't be beat to bring back that "'round-the-campfire" feel.*

- 4 whole chicken breasts, split, skinned, and boned
- Salt to taste (optional)
- 1/4 cup chicken broth
- 1 teaspoon hot pepper sauce
- 1 cup barbecue sauce
- 2 teaspoons dried oregano
- 2 teaspoons ground cumin

Preheat oven to 375°F. Place chicken breasts in a large baking dish; sprinkle with salt, if desired. In a small bowl, combine the chicken broth and hot pepper sauce; pour mixture over chicken. Bake for 20 to 25 minutes, turning once; remove pan from oven. In another small bowl, combine barbecue sauce, oregano, and cumin; brush over chicken. Bake for 10 minutes more or until fully cooked.

NOTE: Serve with flour tortillas, chopped tomatoes and onions, and maybe even sour cream and avocados for a make-your-own buffet.

Chicken with Chunky Sauce

4 servings

When you're feeling adventurous, try this chicken dish with a yummy twist. It'll be fun to keep them guessing about just how you did it!

- 2 whole chicken breasts, split, skinned, and boned
- ¼ cup cornmeal
- 1½ teaspoons dry mustard
- ½ teaspoon nutmeg
- ⅛ teaspoon cayenne pepper
- 1 tablespoon seafood seasoning (to taste)
- 2 to 3 tablespoons vegetable oil

CUCUMBER SAUCE

- 1 bottle (8 ounces) ranch dressing
- 1 medium-sized cucumber, peeled, seeded, and chopped
- 2 scallions, chopped
- ½ teaspoon dried dillweed

Remove the fillet from bottom of each chicken breast half; take out tough white tendon. Cut each chicken breast piece in half lengthwise (do not cut the fillets). (There should be a total of 12 pieces of chicken.) In a large shallow dish, combine the cornmeal, dry mustard, nutmeg, cayenne pepper, and seafood seasoning; dip chicken pieces into mixture. In a skillet, heat the oil until moderately hot; sauté the chicken pieces until golden. Combine all the sauce ingredients in a medium-sized bowl; mix well. Warm (do not cook) the sauce either on the stove or in the microwave, and serve under or over the chicken.

NOTE: This makes about 1⅓ cups cucumber sauce, which you might want to try with other chicken or fish dishes.

Easy Turkey Divan

4 servings

During the cooler months it's time to think of casseroles. We certainly don't mind lighting the stove, and there's something right about a bubbling dish on a winter table. And they're so easy–like Turkey Divan. Sounds fancy, doesn't it? Well, try this!

- 1 pound cooked boneless turkey breast
- 1 package (10 ounces) frozen broccoli spears, thawed
- 1 can (10¾ ounces) condensed cream of mushroom soup
- 1 cup (4 ounces) shredded Swiss cheese
- 2 tablespoons dry sherry
- ⅛ teaspoon nutmeg

Preheat oven to 350°F. Cut turkey into ¼-inch slices; set aside. Coat a 6"x10" baking dish with nonstick vegetable spray. Place the broccoli in the baking dish and top with the turkey slices. In a medium-sized bowl, combine the soup, cheese, sherry, and nutmeg; spread over the turkey. Bake for 30 to 40 minutes, until bubbling and brown.

NOTE: To make this casserole in the microwave, assemble as above. Cover the baking dish with plastic wrap recommended for microwaves and microwave on high for 4 to 5 minutes. Rotate the baking dish and continue cooking on high for 4 to 5 minutes more or until done. Please remember that cooking time may vary slightly according to the wattage of your microwave.

Chicken "Spareribs"

4 main-dish servings

Now you can get the great flavor of restaurant spareribs at home—and with chicken! How about that‽!

- 1 to 2 tablespoons vegetable oil
- 8 chicken thighs, skinned
- ½ cup plus 1 tablespoon water
- ⅓ cup soy sauce
- ⅓ cup light brown sugar, firmly packed
- ¼ cup apple juice
- 2 tablespoons ketchup
- 1 tablespoon cider vinegar
- 1 garlic clove, crushed
- ½ teaspoon crushed red pepper
- ¼ teaspoon ground ginger
- 1 tablespoon cornstarch

In a nonstick skillet, heat oil until moderately hot. Add chicken and lightly brown on all sides for about 6 to 7 minutes, turning frequently. In a large bowl, combine the ½ cup water, soy sauce, light brown sugar, apple juice, ketchup, cider vinegar, garlic, red pepper, and ginger; add to chicken. Bring to a boil, cover, then reduce heat and simmer for 20 minutes. In a small bowl, blend cornstarch and remaining 1 tablespoon water. Add to chicken and cook, stirring, until sauce thickens and glazes chicken pieces.

NOTE: Serve warm as an appetizer or as a main course over hot cooked rice. Garnish with sliced scallions, if desired. For a change, you can even use chicken wings instead of thighs.

Skillet Stew

about 4 servings

It's quick, but it's still got an old-fashioned taste. And by changing the seasonings, you can get a different taste each time: Add a touch of ginger for a trip to the Orient, some oregano and thyme for a trip to the Mediterranean. You get the idea–make your own adventure!

- 2 tablespoons vegetable oil
- 1 medium-sized onion, chopped
- 1 can (14½ ounces) stewed tomatoes
- 3 cups chunked cooked chicken or turkey
- 1 medium-sized green bell pepper, cut into chunks
- 1 can (7 or 8 ounces) whole kernel corn, drained
- ¾ cup picante sauce
- 1 teaspoon ground cumin
- ½ teaspoon salt

In a large skillet, heat the oil; add the onion and cook until tender, about 3 minutes. Add tomatoes, breaking up large pieces with a wooden spoon. Stir in remaining ingredients; simmer for 10 minutes or until green pepper is crisp-tender.

NOTE: Serve plain or over rice. For a change, you might want to add a drained can of garbanzo beans (chick peas) or white beans.

Chicken Parmesan

4 servings

D*elicious . . . but think it's too hard to make at home? Uh-Uh! Not this way!*

- 2 whole chicken breasts, split, skinned, and boned
- 2 cans (14½ ounces each) Italian-style stewed tomatoes
- 2 tablespoons cornstarch
- ½ teaspoon dried oregano
- ¼ cup grated Parmesan cheese

Preheat oven to 425°F. Place chicken breasts in an 8-inch square baking dish that has been coated with nonstick vegetable spray and bake for 15 to 20 minutes. Meanwhile, in a saucepan, combine tomatoes, cornstarch, and oregano; cook over a medium heat, stirring constantly, until sauce thickens. Pour heated sauce over chicken and sprinkle with Parmesan cheese. Bake for 5 minutes more (just long enough to melt the Parmesan cheese).

NOTE: I also like to add a touch of hot pepper sauce, basil, or a sprinkle of garlic. I sometimes top the chicken with mozzarella cheese slices during the last few minutes of baking to make it even more "authentic."

Farm Chicken

4 servings

D*inner the way it was "down on the farm"–only in a lot less time. And wait 'til you hear all that lip-smacking . . . just like from Mama's chicken!*

- 2 tablespoons olive oil
- 1 3- to 3½-pound chicken, cut into 8 pieces
- Salt to taste
- Black pepper to taste
- 1 large green bell pepper, diced
- 1 large onion, diced
- 2 garlic cloves, crushed
- 1 package (10 ounces) frozen peas

In a large skillet, heat the olive oil. Season the chicken with salt and black pepper and place it in the skillet; brown on all sides. Remove the chicken and set aside. Place the green pepper, onion, and garlic in the skillet and cook for about 5 minutes or until softened, stirring frequently. Return the chicken to the skillet, cover, and cook over a medium-low heat for 45 to 50 minutes, stirring often. Gently stir in the frozen peas and cook for another 5 minutes.

NOTE: Serve with potatoes, rice, or noodles.

Fast Chicken

6 servings

"Fast" and "lean" are two of our favorites these days. This will be, too–when you try it you'll see! By the way, the eaters will never in a million years think that "easy" had anything to do with this!

- 1/4 cup vegetable oil
- 2 tablespoons lemon juice
- 1 cup grated Parmesan cheese
- 1/2 cup biscuit baking mix
- 1/4 teaspoon pepper
- 3 whole chicken breasts, split, skinned, boned, and flattened
- 2 tablespoons margarine or butter

In a small bowl, mix the oil and lemon juice. In a shallow bowl, mix the cheese, biscuit mix, and pepper. Dip the chicken in the oil mixture, then coat with the cheese mixture. In a large skillet, heat the margarine over medium heat until hot. Sauté the chicken until golden and done, about 3 to 5 minutes on each side.

NOTE: How about serving it with Russian dressing or sautéed mushrooms⸮! You can use turkey cutlets instead of chicken breasts—they're even "faster" 'cause they don't have to be flattened. Everything works!

Chicken Holiday

8 servings

Even if it isn't a holiday, this taste combination will make it feel like one! Really easy!

- ½ cup vegetable oil
- 2 3- to 4-pound chickens, cut into 8 pieces each
- 1 can (16 ounces) whole-berry cranberry sauce
- 1 can (16 ounces) frozen concentrated orange juice, thawed
- 2 tablespoons firmly packed brown sugar
- 1½ teaspoons salt
- 1 teaspoon prepared mustard
- ½ teaspoon pepper

Preheat oven to 350°F. In a large skillet, heat the oil over medium heat; add the chicken and brown on all sides. Place chicken in a large baking dish or roasting pan. In a medium-sized bowl, stir together the cranberry sauce and orange juice. Add the brown sugar, salt, mustard, and pepper; mix well. Pour cranberry sauce mixture over chicken. Bake for 35 to 45 minutes or until done and a fork can be inserted in the chicken with ease. Turn oven to broil and broil chicken for 5 minutes until browned.

Five-Minute Chicken

4 to 6 servings

P*erfect when you need that special meal in a hurry. It's even rich-tasting, too . . . I promise! Afterward the shock comes when you tell them it took only 5 minutes!*

- 1 2-½- to 3-pound chicken, cut into 8 pieces
- 1 cup mayonnaise
- 1 can (11 ounces) Cheddar cheese soup
- 1 can (about 4 ounces) sliced or button mushrooms
- ½ cup dry white wine
- 1 garlic clove, crushed
- 1 tablespoon dried parsley
- 1 teaspoon curry powder
- Salt to taste
- Pepper to taste
- Paprika for garnish

Preheat oven to 350°F. Coat a 9″x13″ baking dish with nonstick vegetable spray. Arrange the chicken pieces in baking dish; set aside. In a large bowl, mix together the mayonnaise, soup, mushrooms, wine, garlic, parsley, curry powder, salt, and pepper; pour mixture over chicken. Bake for 1 to 1¼ hours, until done. Sprinkle with paprika just before serving.

"White Hat" Chili

6 to 8 servings

Since everybody loves chili, here's a lighter version to make them all happy. Served with lots of fun go-alongs, this is bound to become a regular favorite.

- 2 tablespoons vegetable oil
- 1 medium-sized onion, chopped
- 2 garlic cloves, crushed
- 1 teaspoon ground cumin
- 2 whole chicken breasts, skinned, boned, and cut into 1-inch chunks
- 1 can (15 to 20 ounces) white kidney beans (cannellini), drained
- 1 can (15 to 19 ounces) garbanzo beans, drained
- 1 can (16 to 17 ounces) whole kernel corn, drained
- 2 cans (4 ounces each) chopped mild green chilies
- 1 can (10½ ounces) chicken broth or soup
- Hot pepper sauce to taste

Preheat oven to 350°F. In a small skillet, heat the oil until moderately hot; add onion, garlic, and cumin and sauté just until onion is soft. In a 2½-quart casserole, combine onion mixture with chicken, kidney and garbanzo beans, corn, chilies, and broth; bake for about 1¼ hours or until chicken is tender and cooked through, stirring occasionally. Before serving chili, stir in hot pepper sauce.

NOTE: Serve over cooked rice. For a change, you can use ¼ cup picante sauce instead of the chilies, or prepare a packaged soup mix and use instead of canned soup.

Turkey Joes

6 servings

Remember Sloppy Joes? They were a simple and quick meal that everybody loved. Well, ground turkey really fits today's light tastes, but these work with any type meat or buns. (They're fun eating, too!)

- 2 tablespoons vegetable oil
- 1 pound ground turkey
- 1 cup chopped onion
- ½ cup chopped celery
- ½ cup chopped green bell pepper
- 2 garlic cloves, minced
- 1 can (8 ounces) tomato sauce
- ¼ cup Worcestershire sauce
- ¾ cup water
- 1 teaspoon salt
- Black pepper to taste
- Dash hot pepper sauce (optional)

In a large skillet, heat the oil; add the turkey and brown. Add onion, celery, green pepper, and garlic and sauté for 5 minutes, stirring often. Mix in the remaining ingredients and simmer for 30 minutes.

NOTE: Serve on buttered, toasted buns.

Stuffed Chicken Breasts

12 servings

Want to be a holiday hero? Or even an everyday hero? You can always be a hero because this one's a cinch!

- 1 tablespoon vegetable oil
- 1 onion, finely chopped
- 1 garlic clove, crushed
- 1 package (10 ounces) frozen spinach, thawed and well drained
- 2 tablespoons chopped fresh parsley
- 2 tablespoons chopped fresh basil or 1 teaspoon dried basil
- 1 cup ricotta cheese
- 1/4 cup grated Parmesan cheese
- 1 egg
- Salt to taste
- Pepper to taste
- 6 whole chicken breasts, split and boned (leave skin on)

Preheat oven to 375°F. In a large skillet, heat the vegetable oil until moderately hot; add onion and garlic, cooking just until tender. Stir in spinach, parsley, and basil; heat thoroughly. Remove skillet from heat and let cool to room temperature. In a large bowl, mix together the ricotta and Parmesan cheeses, the egg, salt, and pepper; add the spinach mixture and blend. Place chicken breasts, skin-side up, on a cutting board. Gently loosen skin from one end of each breast, creating a pocket in each. Stuff each pocket with the spinach-cheese mixture and gently press on surface of skin to spread mixture evenly under skin. Tuck ends of skin and meat under the chicken breasts. Place stuffed chicken breasts in a greased baking dish(es) and bake for 35 to 45 minutes or until chicken is done and skin is golden brown. Serve immediately.

NOTE: It's easy to use Stuffed Chicken Breasts as a cold party hors d'oeuvre. Simply cover and refrigerate the cooked breasts until needed; then just before serving, slice into serving-sized pieces.

Chicken Carib

4 servings

Caribbean cooking is one of the current rages in the restaurants. Well, we can make it ourselves for a lot less than them. There's nothing to it–it's easy and delicious, and they'll be raving about the fresh island taste you're serving!

- 1 3- to 4-pound chicken, cut into 8 pieces
- 2 tablespoons butter or margarine
- ½ cup chopped onion
- 1 garlic clove, crushed
- 1 can (8 ounces) tomato sauce
- ¾ cup chicken broth
- ½ cup stuffed green olives, drained and sliced
- ¼ cup light raisins
- 1 tablespoon white vinegar
- ¼ teaspoon chili powder
- ¼ teaspoon allspice
- 1 green bell pepper, cut into strips

In a large skillet, brown the chicken in the butter. Remove chicken; set aside. Add onion and garlic to skillet; cook until lightly browned. Stir in tomato sauce, chicken broth, olives, raisins, vinegar, chili powder, and allspice. Return chicken to skillet; spoon sauce over chicken, cover, and simmer for 30 minutes. Add the green pepper; cover and cook for 10 minutes more or until chicken is fork-tender and no pink is showing.

NOTE: Serve over hot cooked rice. Dark raisins, bottled garlic, or stuffed olive pieces will work just as well.

Chicken and Sunshine

4 servings

How about something that smacks of the Mediterranean tonight? Or the Caribbean? Or Spain? Or anywhere sunny? And how about something quick? And, of course, delicious? Well, here it is!

2 tablespoons olive oil
1 green bell pepper, thinly sliced
⅔ cup sliced scallions
2 whole chicken breasts (about 1 pound) split, skinned, and boned
1 can (14½ ounces) whole tomatoes
1 envelope (0.6 ounces) dry Italian dressing mix
1 tablespoon dried basil

In a large skillet, heat the olive oil until moderately hot; stir in the pepper and scallions. Add chicken and cook until browned. Drain tomatoes, reserving ⅓ cup liquid; add tomatoes and reserved liquid to chicken mixture. Sprinkle Italian dressing mix and basil over top. Reduce heat to low and simmer, covered, for about 20 minutes, until chicken is done.

NOTE: If you use cut-up chicken, it's like a quick Chicken Cacciatore. Garnish or season with your favorites.

Sweet-'n'-Saucy Chicken

4 to 6 servings

You want something easy and quick, but fancy-looking–something you'd be proud to serve to your family or company? Well, we all know how easy stir-frying is.

- 2 tablespoons olive oil
- 2 whole chicken breasts, skinned, boned, and cut into ¾-inch strips
- 2 carrots, thinly sliced
- 1 small onion, thinly sliced
- 1 small green bell pepper, chopped

SAUCE

- 1 cup orange juice
- ½ cup bottled chili sauce
- 2 tablespoons all-purpose flour
- 1 tablespoon firmly packed brown sugar

In a large skillet, heat the olive oil until moderately hot; add the chicken, carrots, onion, and green pepper. Stir-fry until chicken is cooked through and veggies are tender. In a small bowl, mix sauce ingredients; stir sauce into chicken mixture. Bring to a boil, then reduce heat and simmer for 5 to 6 minutes or until sauce thickens, stirring occasionally. Serve immediately.

NOTE: Serve over cooked noodles or rice. This is great made in a wok, too.

Tandoori Chicken

3 to 4 servings

This is a shortcut version to traditional Indian tandoori chicken.

- 1 tablespoon paprika
- 1 tablespoon coriander
- ½ teaspoon ground cardamom
- ½ teaspoon salt
- ½ teaspoon onion powder
- ¼ teaspoon garlic powder
- ¼ teaspoon cayenne pepper
- ¼ teaspoon ground cinnamon
- ⅛ teaspoon chili powder
- Dash turmeric
- 2 tablespoons vegetable oil
- 2 tablespoons water
- 1 tablespoon lemon juice
- 1 3- to 4-pound chicken, cut into 8 pieces

Preheat oven to 350°F. In a bowl, mix together the paprika, coriander, cardamom, salt, onion powder, garlic powder, cayenne pepper, cinnamon, chili powder, and turmeric; stir in the oil, water, and lemon juice. Place the chicken in a 9″x13″ baking dish. Brush the spice mixture generously over the chicken and bake for 1 hour. Turn oven to broil and broil chicken, skin-side up, 4 inches from the source of the heat for 5 to 10 minutes or until golden brown.

Chicken Cacciatore

3 to 4 servings

Here's a real Italian homestyle recipe that's fast and delicious! What could be easier?

- 1/4 cup vegetable oil
- 1 2 1/2 to 3-pound chicken, cut into 8 pieces
- 1 medium-sized onion, sliced
- 1 can (28 ounces) whole tomatoes
- 1/2 cup minced fresh parsley
- 1 teaspoon dried basil
- 1 teaspoon salt
- 1 teaspoon dried oregano
- 1 garlic clove, minced
- 1/4 teaspoon black pepper
- 1/8 teaspoon crushed red pepper
- 1 cup fresh mushrooms or 1 can (about 4 ounces) sliced mushrooms, drained

In a large skillet, heat the oil; add the chicken and brown on all sides. Remove chicken from skillet and set aside. Place onion in skillet and cook in drippings until tender; drain off excess oil, then add remaining ingredients. Return chicken to skillet and simmer for about 40 minutes, uncovered, turning chicken occasionally.

NOTE: This is great served over thin spaghetti.

Cider-Baked Turkey Breast

12 to 16 servings

Yes, turkey breast is the nation's favorite part of the bird—and cider gives it an old-time harvest flavor.

- 1 5- to 6-pound turkey breast
- 1½ cups plus ½ cup apple cider or apple juice
- ¼ cup soy sauce
- 2 tablespoons cornstarch

Preheat oven to 450°F. Place turkey breast, skin-side up, in a large roasting pan. Bake, uncovered, for 30 minutes. Remove turkey from oven and lower temperature to 325°F. In a large bowl, combine the 1½ cups apple cider and the soy sauce; pour mixture over turkey breast. Cover and bake for 1½ to 2 hours more, basting turkey frequently with cider mixture. In a small bowl, combine cornstarch and remaining ½ cup apple cider. Remove turkey from oven and stir cornstarch mixture into pan drippings. Return turkey to oven and bake, uncovered, until sauce is thickened, about 15 to 20 minutes more. Transfer turkey to serving platter and serve with the sauce.

Slow-Cookin' Chicken

4 to 5 servings

Here's one of Mama's favorites from years gone by–an easy, one-pot dinner that can be made simply by putting it on the stove and letting it slow cook. (That's what she did!) And you can add your own family favorite touches!

- 1 4- to 5-pound chicken, cut into 8 pieces
- 1 can (10¾ ounces) cream of chicken soup
- 1 tablespoon prepared mustard
- ½ teaspoon pepper
- ½ teaspoon onion powder
- ½ cup water

Place chicken pieces in a large pot. In a medium-sized bowl, combine the remaining ingredients; mix well. Pour soup mixture over chicken. Bring chicken to a very slow boil; reduce heat and simmer, covered, for 2 hours, stirring occasionally.

NOTE: Serve over rice, noodles, or pasta or with bread for dunking. For a different taste treat, try adding ½ teaspoon of either dillweed, tarragon, caraway, or oregano. You can also add some celery and carrot chunks, or whatever other veggies your family likes.

Chicken Dijon

12 servings

In the mood for an old-time favorite that sounds like fancy-gourmet? Here's how you can serve a really today-type meal that'll make you look like a pro–but quicker, easier, and more exciting!

- 6 whole chicken breasts, split, skinned, and boned
- ⅓ cup Dijon mustard
- 1 teaspoon dried dillweed or 2 to 3 teaspoons chopped fresh dill
- 12 slices Swiss cheese, cut to about the size of the flattened breasts
- 2 eggs, beaten
- 1 cup seasoned bread crumbs
- 2 tablespoons butter or margarine
- 2 tablespoons grated Parmesan cheese

Preheat oven to 350°F. Pound chicken breast pieces until they are ½ inch thick. In a small bowl, combine mustard and dillweed; mix well. Spread mustard mixture evenly over chicken breasts. Top each breast with a slice of Swiss cheese, then tuck and roll them up. Dip chicken breast rolls in the beaten eggs, then in the bread crumbs. Place rolled and coated breasts in a large skillet and sauté in butter until golden brown. Remove breasts from skillet and place in a 9"x13" baking dish that has been coated with nonstick vegetable spray. Sprinkle with the Parmesan cheese and bake for about 25 minutes, until fully cooked.

NOTE: You can also make this dish with chicken or turkey cutlets. Using cutlets is a great way to save time–you don't have to do any pounding. If you prefer, you can use the light versions of the cheeses or butter.

Meats

"What's for dinner?" usually means our main course. It's the center of the plate—the steak, chops, or roast—the part that everybody looks forward to.

Years ago Mama had to go to the butcher every day, and she brought home whatever was most affordable. She could use some of the toughest, cheapest cuts and make them into the richest, most luxurious-tasting meals. Boy, did we look forward to that!

Of course, Mama spent a good part of each day in the kitchen. We can't do that today, so instead we buy what is more appealing and convenient. We can usually pick up something in the market and have it home and ready to go on the table in no time. Or maybe we'll put something together quickly tonight so it's ready to go at dinnertime tomorrow.

Today with our better-than-ever values and our wide variety of choices, we're in for meat main courses that would even delight and amaze Mama!

Timetable for Roasting Large Beef Roasts

To roast beef roasts: Place beef roast, straight from the refrigerator, fat-side up (if present) on a rack in a shallow roasting pan. Rub with herbs or season, if desired. Insert meat thermometer so the tip is centered in the roast but does not touch bone or fat. Always roast without a cover or the addition of liquid; otherwise the meat will be braised. Remove the roast from the oven when the thermometer registers 10 degrees F. lower than desired; the roast will continue to cook as it stands. Allowing the roast to "stand" for 15 to 20 minutes after roasting makes carving easier.

Cut	Approximate Weight (in pounds)	Oven Temperature (in degrees F.)	Final Meat Thermometer Reading (in degrees F.)	Approximate Cooking Time* (minutes per pound)
Beef Rib Roast	8 to 10	300 to 325	140 (rare) 160 (medium)	19 to 21 23 to 25
Beef Rib Eye Roast	8 to 10	350	140 (rare) 160 (medium)	13 to 15 16 to 18
Beef Tenderloin Roast, Whole	4 to 6	425	140 (rare)	45 to 60 (total cooking time)
Beef Round Tip Roast	8 to 10	300 to 325	140 (rare) 160 (medium)	18 to 22 23 to 25
Beef Top Round Roast	6 to 10	300 to 325	140 (rare) 160 (medium)	17 to 19 22 to 24
Beef Top Loin Roast	7 to 9	300 to 325	140 (rare) 160 (medium)	9 to 11 13 to 15

*Cooking times are based on meat taken directly from the refrigerator.

Courtesy of the Meat Board Test Kitchens

Timetable for Roasting Veal

Roasting is the simplest and the most appropriate cooking method for larger cuts of veal from the loin, sirloin, and rib. A boneless veal shoulder arm, eye round, or rump roast also can be roasted successfully in a slow oven.

To roast veal: Place roast (straight from refrigerator), fat-side up, on rack in open shallow roasting pan. Season before or after cooking. Insert meat thermometer into thickest part of roast, not touching bone or fat. Do not add water. Do not cover. Roast in slow oven (300° to 325°F.) until meat thermometer registers 5 degrees below desired doneness. (Oven does not have to be preheated.) Allow roast to stand for 15 to 20 minutes before serving. Temperature will rise about 5 degrees, and roast will be easier to carve.

Roasting at 300° to 325°F.

Cut	Approximate Weight (in pounds)	Final Meat Thermometer Reading (in degrees F.)	Approximate Cooking Time* (minutes per pound)
Loin	3 to 4	160 (medium)	34 to 36
		170 (well)	38 to 40
Loin (boneless)	2 to 3	160 (medium)	18 to 20
		170 (well)	22 to 24
Rib	4 to 5	160 (medium)	25 to 27
		170 (well)	29 to 31
Crown (12 to 14 ribs)	7½ to 9½	160 (medium)	19 to 21
		170 (well)	21 to 23
Rib Eye	2 to 3	160 (medium)	26 to 28
		170 (well)	30 to 33
Rump (boneless)	2 to 3	160 (medium)	33 to 35
		170 (well)	37 to 40
Shoulder (boneless)	2½ to 3	160 (medium)	31 to 34
		170 (well)	34 to 37

*Cooking times are based on meat taken directly from the refrigerator.

Courtesy of the Beef Board and Veal Committee of the Beef Industry Council

Timetable for Roasting Lamb

To roast lamb: Place lamb, fat-side up, on rack in open roasting pan. Insert meat thermometer so bulb is centered in roast and not touching bone or fat. Do not add water. Do not cover. Roast in slow oven (300° to 325°F.) to desired degree of doneness. Season with salt and pepper if desired.

Cut	Approximate Weight (in pounds)	Final Meat Thermometer Reading (in degrees F.)	Approximate Cooking Time* (minutes per pound)
Leg	7 to 9	140 (rare)	15 to 20
		160 (medium)	20 to 25
		170 (well)	25 to 30
Leg	5 to 7	140 (rare)	20 to 25
		160 (medium)	25 to 30
		170 (well)	30 to 35
Leg (boneless)	4 to 7	140 (rare)	25 to 30
		160 (medium)	30 to 35
		170 (well)	35 to 40
Leg, Shank Half	3 to 4	140 (rare)	30 to 35
		160 (medium)	40 to 45
		170 (well)	45 to 50
Leg, Sirloin Half	3 to 4	140 (rare)	25 to 30
		160 (medium)	35 to 40
		170 (well)	45 to 50
Shoulder† (boneless)	3½ to 5	140 (rare)	30 to 35
		160 (medium)	35 to 40
		170 (well)	40 to 45

Note: Cooking times are based on meat taken directly from the refrigerator.

*Oven not preheated.

†For presliced, bone-in shoulder, add 5 minutes per pound to times recommended for boneless shoulder.

Courtesy of the Lamb Committee of the National Live Stock & Meat Board

Timetable for Roasting Pork

To roast pork: Place pork, fat-side up, on rack in open roasting pan. Rub with herbs or season, if desired. Insert meat thermometer so bulb is centered in roast but does not touch bone or fat. Do not add water. Do not cover. Roast in slow oven (300° to 325°F.), unless instructed otherwise, to 5 degrees below recommended degree of doneness. (Roast continues cooking after removal from oven.) Cover roast with foil tent and let stand for 15 to 20 minutes before carving.

Cut	Approximate Weight (in pounds)	Oven Temperature (in degrees F.)	Final Meat Thermometer Reading (in degrees F.)	Approximate Cooking Time (minutes per pound)
Loin, Center (bone in)	3 to 5	325	160 (medium) 170 (well)	20 to 25 26 to 31
Blade Loin/Sirloin (boneless, tied)	2½ to 3½	325	170 (well)	33 to 38
Boneless Rib End–Chef's Prime	2 to 4	325	160 (medium) 170 (well)	26 to 31 28 to 33
Top (double)	3 to 4	325	160 (medium) 170 (well)	29 to 34 33 to 38
Top	2 to 4	325	160 (medium) 170 (well)	23 to 33 30 to 40
Crown	6 to 10	325	170 (well)	20 to 25

(Continued)

Cut	Approximate Weight (in pounds)	Oven Temperature (in degrees F.)	Final Meat Thermometer Reading (in degrees F.)	Approximate Cooking Time (minutes per pound)
Leg				
Whole (bone in)	12	325	170 (well)	23 to 25
Top (inside)	3½	325	170 (well)	38 to 42
Bottom (outside)	3½	325	170 (well)	40 to 45
Blade Boston (boneless)	3 to 4	325	170 (well)	40 to 45
Tenderloin	½ to 1 pound	425	160 (medium) 170 (well)	27 to 29 30 to 32
Backribs		425	tender	1½ to 1¾ hrs.
Country-style Ribs	1" slices	425	tender	1½ to 1¾ hrs.
Spareribs		425	tender	1½ to 1¾ hrs.
Ground Pork Loaf	1 to 1½ pounds	350	170 (well)	55 to 65
Meatballs	1" 2"	350 350	170 (well) 170 (well)	25 to 30 30 to 35

Note: Smaller roasts require more minutes per pound than larger roasts. Cooking times are based on meat taken directly from the refrigerator.

Courtesy of the Meat Board Test Kitchens & Pork Industry Group

Light Beef Stroganoff

4 servings

With everybody watching what they eat these days, wouldn't it be nice if we could eat the things we like and still eat lighter‽ Well, Beef Stroganoff sounds Old World heavy and fancy, but I've changed it a little. I left in the old-fashioned Eastern European taste but made it today smarter!!

- 1 pound lean boneless round steak
- ½ cup chopped onion
- 1 garlic clove, minced
- 1 teaspoon reduced-calorie margarine
- 2 cups sliced mushrooms, fresh or canned
- 3 tablespoons dry red wine
- 1 tablespoon cornstarch
- ¾ cup beef broth
- ¼ teaspoon pepper
- ¼ teaspoon dried dillweed
- 8 ounces plain nonfat yogurt
- 1 pound hot cooked noodles

Partially freeze the steak for easier slicing. Slice it diagonally across the grain into ½-inch slices; set aside. In a large skillet, sauté the onion and garlic in the margarine until tender. Add the steak and mushrooms to skillet; cook, stirring constantly, until steak is browned. Add wine; reduce heat and simmer, covered, for 10 minutes. In a small bowl, dissolve cornstarch in broth; stir broth mixture into steak mixture. Cook, stirring constantly, until smooth and thickened. Remove skillet from heat; stir in pepper, dillweed, and yogurt. Serve over the noodles.

Onion-Crusted Steak

4 servings

P*robably one of the most often-asked questions I get is, "What can I do a little different on the grill?" Well, here's an old-time trick that'll get raves for being different and easy. It tastes like a steak sandwich with crispy onions right in it.*

- 1 can (2.8 ounces) French fried onions
- 1 teaspoon salt
- 1 teaspoon paprika
- ½ teaspoon garlic powder
- 4 steaks, about ¼ to ½ pound each, cut ½ inch thick
- 2 tablespoons vegetable oil

In a blender or food processor or by hand, crush the French fried onions to make crumbs. In a small bowl, stir together the onion crumbs, salt, paprika, and garlic powder. Brush steaks with the oil, dip them in crumb mixture, and place on grill. Cook steaks over high heat to desired degree of doneness, or about 5 minutes per side for medium.

NOTE: Boneless rib eye, strip, or sirloin steaks work just fine. For a change, you can also try hamburger, or pork or lamb chops.

Sweet-and-Sour Pork Chops

4 to 6 servings

For years I looked for the sweet and sour sauce I enjoy so much in Chinese restaurants. THIS IS IT!! It's got the perfect amount of vinegar–not too strong–just right so that everybody loves it. Hooray!! I finally found it!

- 1 can (20 ounces) pineapple chunks, drained, with liquid reserved
- 1¼ cups ketchup
- 1 tablespoon firmly packed brown sugar
- 1 tablespoon cider vinegar
- 3 carrots, sliced into ¼-inch rounds
- ½ green bell pepper, cut into chunks
- 2 tablespoons vegetable oil
- 4 to 6 pork loin chops, 1 inch thick

Preheat oven to 350°F. In a large saucepan, combine reserved pineapple juice, ketchup, brown sugar, and vinegar; cook for 5 minutes, until hot. Add pineapple chunks, carrots, and green pepper; remove from heat. In a large skillet, heat the oil; add chops and brown. In a shallow baking dish, arrange chops; spread pineapple-vegetable mixture over top. Cover with aluminum foil and bake for 1 hour, until chops are done and vegetables are crisp-tender.

NOTE: Serve over rice.

All-in-One Burger

6 to 8 hamburgers

OK, the gang's coming over and we want the burgers to be special. That doesn't have to mean a lot of work, though–you can put all the flavors right in the burgers with just bottled picante sauce!

- 2 pounds ground beef
- ⅓ cup mild picante sauce
- ⅓ cup (1⅓ ounces) shredded Cheddar cheese
- 1 teaspoon pepper

In a large mixing bowl, combine all ingredients. Form mixture into patties; layer the patties in aluminum foil and refrigerate to firm them up. Broil, grill, or bake to desired doneness.

NOTE: Serve with your favorite burger or Tex-Mex toppings or just plain on a bun. You can add your own seasonings or try barbecue sauce instead of picante sauce.

One-Pot "Whatever"

(They love the name–and they know they won't get the recipe from you!)

4 to 6 servings

We're always looking for hearty suppers. You can't go wrong with this one. Everybody's Mama had this one in her bag of tricks. Go ahead–there're no rules. Whatever you throw in is just fine!

- 2 pounds beef (shoulder, round, or chuck steak), cut into bite-sized pieces
- ¼ cup (½ stick) butter or margarine
- 1 medium-sized onion, cut into wedges
- 2 celery stalks, chopped
- 1 cup sliced mushrooms
- 1 garlic clove, crushed
- ¼ teaspoon salt
- ¼ teaspoon pepper
- ½ cup dry red wine
- 2 cans (10½ ounces each) beef broth (or bouillon)

In a large skillet, brown the beef in the butter. Add the onion, celery, mushrooms, garlic, salt, and pepper; reduce heat and simmer for 15 to 20 minutes. Add the wine and broth; cover and simmer for 1 hour or until meat is tender.

NOTE: Serve over noodles, rice, or slices of garlic bread. You can substitute oil for the butter, bottled garlic for the fresh, or use a different wine.

Taco Casserole

about 4 servings

Here's a great beef casserole recipe that combines easy with Tex-Mex, and you can make it beforehand, then just heat it up.

- 1 pound lean ground beef
- 1 small onion, chopped
- ½ teaspoon garlic powder
- 1 envelope (1.25 ounces) taco seasoning mix
- 1 can (8 ounces) tomato sauce
- 1 cup sour cream
- 1 cup cottage cheese
- 2 cups crushed tortilla chips
- 2 cups (8 ounces) grated Monterey Jack cheese

Preheat oven to 350°F. In a skillet, brown the beef, then drain off excess fat; remove from heat. Add onion, garlic powder, taco seasoning mix, and tomato sauce to beef; mix and set aside. In a medium-sized bowl, combine sour cream and cottage cheese; set aside. Place half the crushed chips in the bottom of a 2½-quart casserole dish that has been coated with a nonstick vegetable spray. Add enough meat mixture to cover the chips, then cover the meat with half the sour cream mixture. Sprinkle with half the grated cheese. Repeat layers. Bake, uncovered, for 30 to 35 minutes, until cheese melts and casserole is heated through.

NOTE: This is just as good made with ground turkey as it is with beef.

"Mixed-Up" Garlic-Braised Lamb Shanks

8 to 12 servings

Let's look at an "old" that has a lot of "new" about it–lamb shanks. And the reason we say they're "mixed up" is 'cause nobody knows if the recipe was originally Armenian, Italian, or Greek. The shanks taste so good you'll see why everybody wants the credit!

- 12 lamb shanks
- ½ cup all-purpose flour
- 1½ teaspoons dried thyme
- 1 tablespoon paprika
- 1 teaspoon salt
- ½ teaspoon dried rosemary
- ⅓ cup vegetable oil
- 4 to 6 garlic cloves, minced, or ½ teaspoon granulated garlic
- 3 cups chicken or beef broth or stock (or water, if desired)
- 1 cup finely chopped onions (optional)

Preheat oven to 350°F. In a shallow bowl, combine flour, thyme, paprika, salt, and rosemary. Dredge lamb shanks in seasoned flour. In a large skillet, heat oil; brown shanks. Place lamb shanks in a baking pan (or pans) in a single layer; sprinkle the remaining flour mixture and garlic on the shanks, add broth and onions, and braise for 1½ hours. Remove from oven and cool; skim off the fat that has risen to the top. Cook for 2 hours more or until tender; serve.

NOTE: If you'd like leaner shanks, after cooking, cool the shanks slightly, refrigerate them, and the next day, remove the solidified fat. Reheat the shanks for an hour, then serve.

Mexican Meat Loaf

4 servings

More Mexican?? You bet!! It's the new popular with the taste of the old country.

- 1½ pounds ground beef
- 1 medium-sized onion, chopped
- ½ cup chopped mushrooms
- ¼ cup chopped green bell pepper
- ½ cup taco sauce
- 2 tablespoons barbecue sauce
- 1 egg, beaten
- ½ cup finely crushed tortilla chips
- ½ teaspoon salt
- Dash black pepper

Preheat oven to 400°F. In a large bowl, combine all ingredients; mix well. Pack meat mixture into a greased 8"x4" loaf pan. Bake for 1¼ hours or until done.

NOTE: You can use ground veal, pork, or turkey, if you prefer. You can also use ketchup instead of barbecue sauce and, for a change, you can melt some Cheddar cheese on top of the meat loaf during the last 10 minutes of baking.

Country-Fried Steak

about 3 servings

Remember the food of the '50s—the diner food, the country food, the real stick-to-your-ribs stuff? This one will bring you back, but without all the fussing!

- 1½ pounds cubed steak
- ½ cup Italian salad dressing
- ½ cup vegetable oil
- ½ cup all-purpose flour
- Salt to taste
- Pepper to taste

Cut cubed steak into individual-sized portions and place in a large bowl. Pour the Italian dressing over the steak pieces and toss well. Place the flour in a plastic bag or dish; add steak pieces and coat well. In a heavy skillet, heat the oil; fry the steak pieces in oil, turning to brown both sides. Then fry the steak for approximately 2 minutes more per side or until a golden brown crust has formed. Before serving, add salt and pepper to taste.

NOTE: Serve over mashed potatoes, if you like. You can also try this recipe with hamburger, or chicken, turkey, or veal cutlets, instead of steak. Instead of Italian dressing you can try your favorite salad dressing—creamy, plain, or light—and any other seasonings that will give it your own special touch.

Dijon Honey Chops

4 servings

These are as fine, fancy-tasting, and mouth-watering as any pork chops I've ever had. And we can end up looking that fine and fancy in just minutes–WOW!! This one will become one of your standards that they'll always be looking for. It's probably my favorite "new way" with "old-way" pork chops.

- 1¼ to 1½ pounds pork loin chops, ¾ inch thick
- Seasoned salt for sprinkling
- 1 tablespoon vegetable oil
- ⅓ cup orange juice
- 1½ tablespoons Dijon mustard
- 1 tablespoon honey
- 2 teaspoons cornstarch

Sprinkle both sides of chops liberally with seasoned salt. In a large skillet, heat oil; brown chops, about 2 minutes per side. In a bowl, combine remaining ingredients; pour mixture over chops. Cover skillet, reduce heat to low, and simmer for 8 to 10 minutes or until done.

Jamaican Steak

6 servings

One of the popular tastes to hit the country lately is Caribbean. It sounds so exotic and difficult but it's not–it's just delicious! So why not take your family on a Jamaican holiday without leaving home. Ready??

- 1/3 cup lime juice (fresh is best, about 3 limes)
- 1 teaspoon grated lime peel
- 1/4 cup vegetable oil
- 1/4 cup honey
- 2 tablespoons prepared mustard
- 2 garlic cloves, minced
- 1/2 teaspoon salt
- 1/2 teaspoon pepper
- 2 pounds top round, sirloin, or flank steak
- Lime wedges for garnish

In a small bowl, whisk together all ingredients, except steak and lime wedges. Score steak across top or pierce several times with a fork. Place steak in a shallow glass baking dish and pour lime juice mixture over the steak; turn to coat both sides. Refrigerate for 6 to 8 hours to "marry" the flavors, turning occasionally. Remove the steak from the marinade and grill for 5 to 6 minutes on each side (or broil in the oven for 3 minutes on each side), or to desired doneness. Slice thinly on the diagonal and serve with the lime wedges.

NOTE: It's fine to use bottled garlic instead of fresh.

Pepper Steak Stir-Fry

about 6 servings

It's the easiest, fastest, and soon-to-be everybody's favorite 'cause it combines fast Chinese wok cooking with a smack of popular Mexican. My gosh!! Can't do anything but win raves. And when so much of your seasoning comes from a jar, it sure makes it a lot easier.

- ¼ cup vegetable oil
- 2 pounds boneless steak, sliced into thin strips
- 1 large onion, cut into ¾-inch angled slices
- 3 green bell peppers, cut into strips
- ½ pound mushrooms, sliced
- 1½ cups mild picante sauce
- 1 cup water
- ⅓ cup soy sauce
- 3 tablespoons cornstarch
- ¼ teaspoon garlic powder

In a large skillet or wok, heat the oil over high heat until moderately hot; sauté steak and onion for about 5 minutes, stirring often. Add peppers and mushrooms and cook for about 5 minutes more, stirring often, until vegetables are tender. In a bowl, combine picante sauce, water, soy sauce, cornstarch, and garlic powder; add to steak and vegetable mixture. Cook for 2 to 3 minutes more or until the sauce thickens, stirring occasionally.

NOTE: Serve over rice or fried noodles. For an Oriental twist, try using ginger or five-spice powder; for Mexican, try a touch of chili powder or cumin; for Mediterranean, add a little oregano. You can also use different veggies for variety. And here's a hint to make the meat easier to slice: place it in the freezer until firm.

One-Pot Short Ribs

about 4 servings

Nothing's more welcome or down-home any time of the year than an old-fashioned thick-with-barley-and-potatoes short ribs dinner. Remember that? Every Eastern European–influenced home had its own special touch. Ours was to use a bottled teriyaki sauce instead of Worcestershire. (We originally tried it that way because we'd run out of Worcestershire sauce!) And wait'll you see how easy it is!

- 3 pounds beef short ribs
- 1 medium-sized onion, chopped (about 1 cup)
- 3 cups water
- 2 teaspoons paprika
- 2 teaspoons salt
- ¼ teaspoon pepper
- 3 tablespoons teriyaki sauce
- 2 large potatoes, peeled and cut into ½-inch slices
- ½ cup barley

In a large pot, combine the short ribs, onion, water, paprika, salt, pepper, and teriyaki sauce; bring to a boil. Reduce heat to low; cover and cook for about 1½ hours, stirring occasionally. Add the potatoes and barley; cook for an additional hour, stirring occasionally and adding more water, if necessary.

NOTE: This is one of those better-when-reheated-the-next-day recipes. Yup! And reheating in the microwave is fine.

Not-Your-Regular Brisket

about 6 servings

We're usually looking for another way to roast a brisket of beef. Well, here's something a little different for a change. Even with the soy sauce to fool everybody, this is a true "touch of sweet" German and Dutch holiday-style treat.

- 3½ to 4 pounds beef brisket, trimmed
- ½ cup water
- ¼ cup soy sauce
- ¼ teaspoon black pepper
- ¼ cup chopped onion
- 1 green bell pepper, sliced
- ½ cup raisins
- 2 tablespoons brown sugar
- 1 can (20 ounces) unsweetened apple slices, drained

Place brisket in a large pot or baking pan. Add water, soy sauce, and pepper; cover and simmer for 2½ to 3 hours. Add onion, green pepper, raisins, brown sugar, and apple slices; simmer for 30 to 40 minutes more. Remove brisket and slice. Serve, covered with pan juices.

NOTE: You can substitute a couple of sliced fresh apples for the canned. You can also add a touch of hot pepper sauce or garlic to "heat up" the recipe.

Barbecued Steak Strips

3 to 4 servings

W*hen you miss that BBQ flavor because of the weather (or the seasons), just try this sure-fire recipe indoors. It's a winner, even without the grill!*

- 1 pound round or shoulder steak
- 1 tablespoon vegetable oil
- ½ cup ketchup
- 1 teaspoon prepared mustard
- 1 teaspoon chili powder
- 1 teaspoon Worcestershire sauce
- 1 teaspoon instant minced onion
- ½ cup dry red wine

Trim fat from steak and freeze slightly for easier slicing; cut steak into thin strips. In a large skillet, heat the oil; brown steak strips on both sides. Add remaining ingredients; cover and cook slowly for about 1 hour or until tender, adding a little more wine as the liquid cooks out. When the sauce is fairly thick, steak should be tender.

NOTE: Serve on rolls or over rice or noodles. To "heat up" the recipe a bit, you can add cumin, Creole seasoning, or garlic powder.

Mexican Pot Roast

8 servings

A *simple pot roast Mexican style that'll have the gang glad for that little change from the regular ho-hum!*

- 2 tablespoons olive oil
- 4 pounds lean boneless chuck pot roast
- 1 can (14½ ounces) whole tomatoes
- 1 can (3 ounces) chopped green chilies
- 1 envelope (1.25 ounces) taco seasoning mix
- 1 tablespoon beef or chicken dry bouillon granules
- 1 teaspoon sugar
- Onion or garlic powder (optional)

In a Dutch oven (or similar type pot), heat olive oil; brown the pot roast on all sides. In a bowl, combine remaining ingredients; pour over pot roast. Cover and simmer over low heat for 3½ to 4 hours or until pot roast is tender. Slice and serve.

NOTE: Serve with noodles or rice.

Grilled Honey-Garlic Pork Chops

5 to 12 servings

W*ant something a little different to do with pork chops? Well, here's the ticket 'cause the Pennsylvania Dutch sweet and sour touch is the star of the table. You'll see!!*

MARINADE

- 3/4 cup lemon juice
- 3/4 cup honey
- 6 tablespoons soy sauce
- 3 tablespoons dry sherry or any dry white wine
- 6 garlic cloves, chopped

- 10 to 12 pork chops, cut 1½ inches thick

Combine marinade ingredients in a baking dish. Add chops to marinade. Cover and refrigerate overnight, turning once to "marry" the flavors. Remove chops from marinade and grill for about 10 minutes per side or until done. Discard excess marinade.

NOTE: I prefer to use center cut loin chops for a special meal, but rib chops will work just as well, too.

Exotic Lamb-Stuffed Potatoes

6 to 8 servings

I've often said that the spice rack can be an easy world journey. If you want proof, try this little trip we can take to the Middle East!

- 6 to 8 potatoes, baked
- 1¼ pounds ground lamb
- 1 cup chopped onion
- 1 can (28 ounces) whole tomatoes, undrained
- ¼ cup chopped green bell pepper
- ¼ cup chopped fresh parsley
- 1 teaspoon allspice
- ½ teaspoon nutmeg
- Salt to taste
- Black or cayenne pepper to taste

Slice off tops of baked potatoes; scoop out insides and reserve for other uses. In a large skillet, sauté lamb and onion over medium heat until slightly browned. Add tomatoes, green pepper, parsley, allspice, nutmeg, salt, and pepper and cook for 5 to 6 minutes. Preheat oven to 300°F. Place potato shells in a baking pan; spoon meat-tomato mixture into potato shells and heat for about 10 minutes or until heated through. Serve.

NOTE: Ground beef and ground turkey work just as well. I save the insides of the potatoes for potato soup, mashed potatoes, or other potato dishes.

Texas-Style Pot Roast

6 to 8 servings

H*ow about something hearty, and rich and tangy, too? It's a super way to have a hale and hearty meal anytime! This is probably one of the simplest pot roasts ever. But the taste! Oh, the taste!!*

- 1 4- to 5-pound single-cut beef brisket, well trimmed
- 4 cups barbecue sauce
- 2 large onions, thinly sliced
- 1 teaspoon chopped garlic

Preheat oven to 350°F. Place the brisket in a large roasting pan and set aside. In a large saucepan, combine remaining ingredients to make sauce; heat through. Pour 2 cups of the heated sauce over the brisket. Refrigerate remaining sauce for later use. Cook the brisket for 3 to 3½ hours or until tender; cover halfway through that time. Leave in pan and cool brisket in refrigerator; remove all the fat that rises and solidifies on the top. Combine the juices from the roasting pan with the cooled reserved sauce; warm through. Rewarm brisket, slice thinly, and serve topped with warm sauce.

NOTE: Enjoy sliced brisket on rolls, topped with sauce.

Oriental Pork Burgers

4 burgers

Amazing!!! This is one of the best ground pork recipes I've ever made. The Chinese touches make it so flavorful.

- 3 tablespoons soy sauce
- 3 tablespoons wine vinegar
- 2 tablespoons firmly packed brown sugar
- 1 teaspoon ground ginger
- 2 garlic cloves, crushed
- 1 pound ground pork
- 1 large onion, sliced
- ¾ cup water, divided
- 4 teaspoons cornstarch

In a large bowl, combine the soy sauce, wine vinegar, brown sugar, ginger, and garlic. Combine 3 tablespoons of the soy sauce mixture with the pork, reserving the remaining liquid. Form pork into patties and grill until done, about 15 minutes. Meanwhile, pour reserved soy sauce mixture into a saucepan; add onion and cook until it is tender and brown. Add ¼ cup of the water. In a small bowl, mix cornstarch with remaining ½ cup water; pour into saucepan to thicken mixture. Pour soy sauce mixture over cooked burgers and serve.

Salisbury Steak

12 patties

It seems everybody's rediscovering Salisbury Steak these days. There are thousands of ways to prepare it. Basically, it's a hamburger with an onion-flavored gravy, the way Mama used to make it. And is it ever still delicious! (I think they called it "steak" so we'd think we were getting something different from our regular hamburger.)

- 1½ pounds ground beef
- 1½ cups dry bread crumbs
- 2 eggs
- 1½ cups canned carrots, drained and chopped (1 16-ounce can contains about 2 cups)
- 1 small onion, chopped
- ¼ cup milk
- 1½ teaspoons salt
- ¼ teaspoon pepper
- 1 can (10¾ ounces) cream of mushroom soup
- All-purpose flour for coating
- Vegetable oil for browning

GRAVY

- 1 can (4 ounces) mushroom pieces
- 1 can (10¾ ounces) cream of mushroom soup
- 10¾ ounces milk (1 soup can)

In a large bowl, mix the ground beef, bread crumbs, eggs, carrots, onion, milk, salt, pepper, and one can mushroom soup; form mixture into patties. Place flour in a shallow dish; dust patties with flour. In 2 large skillets, heat oil; brown patties on both sides. Drain off excess fat. Sprinkle mushroom pieces over patties. In a medium-sized bowl, combine the remaining 1 can mushroom soup and milk; pour soup-milk mixture evenly over patties. Cook slowly in covered skillets for 25 minutes.

NOTE: Salisbury Steak sure is easy with canned carrots, but fresh carrots work well, too. If you'd like, you can add a little garlic, sage, caraway, or dill to perk up the flavor. For a different taste treat, you can use ground sausage; for a light change you can use ground turkey. You can use a soup mix if you don't have canned cream of mushroom soup; it'll work well, too. You see, anything goes!

Easy Spring Lamb

4 to 6 servings

Here's an old-time tradition that's a lot easier than it used to be because of American spring lambs, which are younger and always mild and tender.

- 1 3-pound boneless leg of lamb
- 1 cup dry red wine
- 1/4 cup Italian salad dressing
- 2 teaspoons dried rosemary leaves
- 1/2 teaspoon garlic powder
- 1/2 teaspoon dry mustard
- 1/2 teaspoon salt
- 1/2 teaspoon pepper

In a large baking dish, mix together all ingredients, except lamb. Place lamb in baking dish and marinate in refrigerator for 2 to 3 hours, turning occasionally. Preheat oven to 350°F. Remove marinade from baking dish; discard marinade. Roast lamb, uncovered, for 1 1/2 to 2 hours or until done.

Peppered Lamb Shanks

6 servings

H*ere's a main course that fits today's desire for economical and easy with an old-time taste that keeps the economical part a secret—they'll never know!*

- 6 lamb shanks
- Salt to taste
- Black pepper to taste
- ¾ cup chicken or beef broth
- 1 yellow bell pepper, sliced
- 1 red bell pepper, sliced
- 1 green bell pepper, sliced
- 1 bunch scallions, sliced
- 1 cup dry white wine
- 1 garlic clove, crushed
- 2 tablespoons cornstarch
- 2 tablespoons water

Preheat oven to 350°F. Sprinkle lamb shanks with salt and pepper; place in a large baking dish. Bake for 2 to 2½ hours, until meat is tender; drain. In a large skillet, combine the broth, peppers, scallions, wine, and garlic; cook just until peppers are tender. Meanwhile, in a small bowl, mix cornstarch and water together. Add cornstarch mixture to the skillet and cook until liquid thickens. Pour pepper mixture over shanks in baking dish and bake for 10 minutes more to heat through.

Chuck Wagon Buns

4 servings

Food tastes special when we're camping out under the stars. But even if we're staying home, we can still capture some of that wonderful open-air flavor right from our kitchen stove–uh, sorry–I mean from the chuck wagon!

- 1 pound ground beef
- ⅔ cup ketchup
- 1 tablespoon firmly packed brown sugar
- 1 tablespoon chili powder
- 1 teaspoon cumin
- ½ teaspoon pepper
- ¼ cup hickory-flavored bottled barbecue sauce
- 4 hot dog rolls
- Butter or margarine for rolls (optional)

In a large skillet, brown the beef; drain off liquid. Stir in ketchup, brown sugar, chili powder, cumin, pepper, and barbecue sauce; simmer for 10 minutes to blend all the flavors. Meanwhile, butter the rolls and toast them under the broiler. Spoon the beef mixture onto the toasted hot dog rolls.

NOTE: Serve with baked beans, pasta salad, or crunchy raw vegetables to complete the meal.

Veal Marsala

3 to 4 servings

This proves we can cook very "hoo hoo" fancy-sounding dishes simply. And with only 6 ingredients, it's done in minutes. And yes, we still have loads of room for our own special touches.

All-purpose flour for coating
¼ teaspoon salt
⅛ teaspoon pepper
1½ pounds veal cutlets, sliced and flattened to ½-inch thickness
8 tablespoons (1 stick) butter or margarine
1 cup Marsala or other red wine

In a shallow dish, mix together the flour, salt, and pepper; coat the veal slices well with the mixture. In a large skillet, sauté the veal slices in the butter over medium-high heat until lightly golden, without stacking or overlapping them. Pour wine into skillet and cook veal for another 2 minutes to warm everything through. Serve immediately.

NOTE: This is just as easy and good made with turkey cutlets or skinless and boneless chicken breasts.

Honey Apple Chops

4 servings

This is the perfect marinade for pork chops on the grill. It tastes like we have a better-than-anybody's secret. Too good to be simple? Hah! Hah! You'll see!

- 1½ cups apple cider or juice
- ¼ cup lemon juice
- ¼ cup soy sauce
- 2 tablespoons honey
- 1 garlic clove, minced
- ¼ teaspoon pepper
- 4 boneless pork loin chops, 1 inch thick

In a bowl, combine all ingredients, except chops; mix well to make a marinade. Place chops in a shallow dish; pour marinade over chops, cover, and refrigerate, turning occasionally, for 4 to 24 hours. Heat grill and grill chops for 10 to 12 minutes, turning once and basting occasionally with marinade. Discard remaining marinade.

Fajitas

4 servings

It's so easy to make these your own "secret recipe"–you may want to change the marinade flavorings or the veggie combinations or even add your own toppings. Whatever you do, you can't go wrong with these fun and trendy all-in-one pockets.

- 1 skirt or flank steak (about 1 to 1½ pounds)
- ¼ cup lime juice
- ¼ cup olive oil
- 2 garlic cloves, crushed
- 1 tablespoon vegetable oil
- 4 flour tortillas (10-inch size), warmed
- 1 cup (4 ounces) shredded Cheddar cheese
- 1 cup shredded lettuce
- 1 tomato, chopped
- 1 small green bell pepper, cut into thin strips
- 2 scallions, sliced
- 2 avocados, seeded, peeled, and sliced
- Sour cream for topping (optional)
- Bottled salsa for topping (optional)

Partially freeze the steak for easier slicing. Slice steak across the grain into ½-inch strips. In a large bowl, mix the lime juice, olive oil, and garlic. Add meat; cover and refrigerate for at least 1 hour, turning occasionally (overnight is best). In a large skillet, heat the vegetable oil; fry meat quickly over medium-high heat until browned. Remove from heat. Fill each tortilla with about ¾ cup meat. Divide cheese, lettuce, tomato, green pepper, scallions, and avocado slices among the tortillas. Serve with sour cream and salsa, if desired.

Vegetable Beef Chili

6 servings

You talk about a whole meal?? How about having your meat and veggies all in one, and all in one pot? Now that's easy!

- ¼ cup vegetable oil
- 1 large onion, chopped
- 1 green bell pepper, chopped
- 1 cup chopped celery
- 3 garlic cloves, minced
- 2 pounds ground beef
- 3 fresh tomatoes, chopped
- 3 tablespoons chili powder
- 2 teaspoons salt
- 1 teaspoon dried oregano
- ¼ teaspoon cayenne pepper, or to taste
- 1 can (15 ounces) red kidney beans (optional)
- 1 cup (4 ounces) grated Cheddar cheese (optional)

In a large pot, heat the oil; sauté the onion, green pepper, celery, and garlic just until tender. Add beef and brown; drain liquid. Add tomatoes, chili powder, salt, oregano, and red pepper; mix. Cover and simmer for 1 hour, stirring occasionally. If desired, add kidney beans during the last 5 minutes of cooking. Serve topped with grated Cheddar cheese, if desired.

Summer Grilled Steak

4 to 6 servings

Here's a quick marinade that's great for when we're short of time or just want a full-flavored steak to light up their eyes. That old-time taste of Mama's long-cooked steak is as close as our barbecue grill.

- ½ cup tomato sauce
- 1 tablespoon olive oil
- 2 tablespoons red wine vinegar
- ½ teaspoon dried oregano
- ¼ teaspoon garlic powder
- ¼ teaspoon salt (optional)
- ¼ teaspoon pepper
- 2 pounds sirloin steak, about ½-inch thick

Preheat the barbecue grill or the oven to broil. In a small bowl, combine all ingredients, except steak; stir well to blend. Prick both sides of the steak with a fork, then place in a shallow baking dish. Brush tomato sauce mixture generously over both sides of steak. Grill or broil for 8 to 10 minutes, then turn, brush on remaining sauce, and cook for 8 to 10 minutes more, to desired doneness. Serve immediately.

NOTE: Serve it your favorite way—sliced, rolled, sandwiched, or pocketed. You can also try porterhouse, rib steak, or top round. For an added zip, try some hot pepper sauce.

Fish and Seafood

Fish sure is popular these days! It *should* be! With all of us being more aware and watching our cholesterol intake, it makes sense!

We're eating lots more fish than ever in restaurants, yet only slightly more at home. I guess many people still think it takes lots of handling and that it smells up our kitchens too much. Well, not true anymore because our fish gets to us fresher than ever. (And when it's frozen at sea, just hours out of the water, it's even fresher than "fresh fish.")

Our selections of mild-flavored fish could even be called "fast food" because they're cooked in minutes. None of that baking for hours 'til it's dry and falls apart, like Mama did it. Nope! Cook it no more than 10 minutes per inch at its thickest part and it'll be moist, tender, and flavorful every time.

And, speaking of flavor, most mild-fleshed fish gets its flavor from our seasonings, so do your own thing. Start with my suggestions, add more or less of those, or add your favorites totally. It'll still be fast and simple . . . and fun getting all that applause!

Parmesan Baked Fish

3 to 4 servings

Fish is a fast food! It takes only minutes no matter how it's cooked–broiled, baked, fried, whatever. This one's a winner for adding a fine, elegant taste without any extra work.

- 1 pound fish fillets
- 1/3 cup all-purpose flour
- 1/4 teaspoon onion powder
- 1/8 teaspoon salt
- 1/8 teaspoon pepper
- 1/2 teaspoon dried dillweed
- 2 tablespoons (1/4 stick) butter or margarine, melted
- 2 tablespoons grated Parmesan cheese

Preheat oven to 450°F. In a shallow bowl, combine the flour, onion powder, salt, pepper, and dillweed; dredge fish fillets in mixture. Coat a shallow baking dish with nonstick vegetable spray; place fish in baking dish. Drizzle melted butter over fish, then sprinkle with Parmesan cheese. Bake for 7 to 10 minutes (depending upon the thickness of the fish) or until fish flakes easily when tested with a fork.

NOTE: Serve with lemon, lime, orange, or grapefruit slices. Instead of flour, try crushed crackers and add fresh ground herbs, if you have some on hand. Haddock, cod, or sole fillets work well.

Very Fancy Fish

4 to 6 servings
(2 cups sauce)

H*ere's a fast, easy way to prepare fish for company. It'll look and taste like the Ritz!*

4 to 6 medium-sized fish fillets (sole, haddock, or cod)

SAUCE

1 cup mild barbecue sauce
1 cup canned crushed tomatoes
⅓ cup finely minced onion
1 teaspoon hot pepper sauce
1 teaspoon Worcestershire sauce
½ teaspoon salt
½ teaspoon garlic powder
½ teaspoon dried oregano
½ teaspoon dried thyme
2 tablespoons dry red wine

Fry, broil, or bake fish fillets until done; set aside. Place all sauce ingredients in a saucepan and mix well; bring to a boil over medium-high heat. Reduce heat and simmer for 2 to 3 minutes more to blend the flavors. Place sauce on a platter and arrange cooked fish on top of it. Serve warm.

Buttermilk Fried Fish

4 to 6 servings

"The batter won't stick!" I hear that all the time. Well, here's a little trick that will hold the batter on and *mellow the fish–all at the same time!*

- 2 pounds white-fleshed fish fillets
- 1 cup buttermilk
- 1 cup biscuit baking mix
- 1 teaspoon salt
- Vegetable oil for frying (1/4 inch deep in large skillet)

Thaw the fish if frozen. Cut fish into serving-sized portions and place in a shallow dish. Pour buttermilk over fish, cover, and refrigerate for 30 minutes, turning once. In a large bowl, combine biscuit mix and salt; remove fish from buttermilk and coat with biscuit mix mixture. In a large skillet, heat oil; place fish in skillet in single layer and cook until it is browned on both sides and flakes easily with a fork. Drain fish on paper towels and serve.

NOTE: Cod, perch, and haddock work especially well.

Chinese Ginger Fish Fillets

4 servings

Know what makes the fish in the Chinese restaurant seem so exotic? It's the ginger! It's so simple that we can enjoy that style fish at home (for a lot less money, too).

BATTER

- 4 eggs, beaten
- 3 tablespoons soy sauce
- 2 tablespoons cornstarch
- 1/4 teaspoon pepper
- 1/4 teaspoon onion powder
- 1/4 teaspoon ground ginger

- 2 pounds white-fleshed fish fillets
- Cornstarch for dipping
- 2 tablespoons peanut oil

SAUCE

- 1 tablespoon sesame oil
- 1 green bell pepper, cut into 1/4-inch slices
- 1 red bell pepper, cut into 1/4-inch slices

In a small bowl, combine batter ingredients; set aside. Dip fillets in cornstarch and then in batter. Reserve remaining batter. In a large nonstick skillet, heat peanut oil; sauté fillets until golden. Remove fillets from skillet and set aside. Add sauce ingredients and reserved batter to same skillet, quick-stirring for 1 minute; serve over fillets.

NOTE: Flounder, cod, and grouper work especially well.

Scalloped Seafood Casserole

6 appetizer or 2 to 3 main-dish servings

Here's a great way to make imitation crabmeat taste very rich! As a main course, surrounded by veggies, it's the way our Mamas would have served it to solve our Sunday night "What-do-I-feel-like?" dilemma.

- 5 tablespoons butter, divided
- 4 tablespoons all-purpose flour
- 2 cups milk
- ½ teaspoon Worcestershire sauce
- 2 tablespoons chopped fresh parsley
- Dash of pepper
- Dash of paprika
- 2 tablespoons sherry
- 2 cups imitation crabmeat pieces (about 1 pound)
- ¼ cup dry bread crumbs

Preheat oven to 350°F. In a large skillet, melt 4 tablespoons butter over medium heat; add flour and stir until smooth paste forms. Add milk; cook for a few minutes until thickened, stirring constantly. Mix in the Worcestershire sauce, parsley, pepper, paprika, and sherry. Place mixture in a well-greased 2-quart casserole. Cover with imitation crabmeat pieces. Make soft buttered bread crumbs by melting the remaining 1 tablespoon butter and mixing with the bread crumbs. Sprinkle over crabmeat pieces. Bake for 20 minutes, until lightly golden.

NOTE: Shrimp and real crabmeat work well, too. Serve over toast points.

Fish French Style

4 servings

***H**ere's a great old way with fish that has it tasting as if it was prepared in a gourmet restaurant. Don't worry! It's really easy!*

- 2 medium-sized onions, finely chopped
- 2 tablespoons butter or margarine
- 4 apples, peeled, cored, and sliced
- 2 cups apple cider or apple juice
- 2 teaspoons cider vinegar
- ½ teaspoon salt
- ½ teaspoon pepper
- 6 white-fleshed fish fillets (about 2 pounds)

Preheat oven to 400°F. In a large skillet, sauté onions in butter just until soft. Add apples, apple cider, vinegar, salt, and pepper; cook until warmed through, about another 1 to 2 minutes. In a 9″ × 13″ baking dish, arrange fillets in a single layer; pour apple mixture over fillets. Cover baking dish with foil and bake for 12 to 15 minutes (depending on the thickness of the fillets) or until fish flakes easily with a fork.

NOTE: Serve with rice or pasta. Garnish with parsley, if desired.

Scalloped Salmon and Corn

6 to 8 servings

Looking for something a little bit different to serve for lunch, brunch, or a light dinner? This'll make them sit up and take notice! Mama could do a million things with a can of salmon; this one proves it 'cause it's one of her best.

- 1 can (6½ ounces) pink salmon, drained and flaked (reserve liquid in measuring cup)
- Milk (enough to make 1 cup when added to salmon liquid)
- 3 tablespoons margarine, divided
- ½ cup chopped onion
- ¼ cup chopped green bell pepper
- 1¼ cups crushed saltine crackers, divided
- 1 can (16 ounces) cream-style corn
- 2 eggs, slightly beaten
- 1 cup (4 ounces) shredded sharp Cheddar cheese
- ¼ teaspoon salt
- ¼ teaspoon black pepper

Preheat oven to 350°F. Add milk to reserved salmon liquid to make 1 cup. In a skillet, melt 2 tablespoons margarine; sauté onion and green pepper until tender. Stir in salmon, milk mixture, 1 cup cracker crumbs, corn, eggs, Cheddar cheese, salt, and pepper; turn into an 8-inch square baking pan coated with nonstick vegetable spray. Melt remaining 1 tablespoon margarine; toss remaining ¼ cup cracker crumbs with melted margarine and sprinkle mixture over casserole. Bake for about 45 minutes or until a knife inserted in the center comes out clean.

NOTE: Sprinkle with parsley, if desired, and serve on white bread toast.

Fish Cakes

about 6 patties

***H**ow about a new way to make an old recipe even better than it was way back when? Remember fish cakes? We can make them easily, and if we have leftover fish from last night's supper—Wow!—it's perfect for this.*

- About ¾ pound cooked white-fleshed fish fillets (cod or sole)
- 2 cups mashed potatoes
- 1 small onion, finely chopped
- 1½ teaspoons salt
- ½ teaspoon pepper
- 1 to 2 eggs, well beaten
- Cornflake crumbs for dredging

Preheat oven to 400°F. In a large bowl, break fish apart and mash. Mix in the potatoes and onion. Form mixture into patties; dip patties in the egg, then the cornflake crumbs. Place coated patties in a baking dish that has been coated with nonstick vegetable spray and bake for about 10 minutes.

NOTE: Adding a little chopped fresh dill or parsley gives these a nice touch. And you can even use instant mashed potatoes here . . . that makes it even easier.

Cheesy Baked Fish

6 servings

We're always looking for a new way to jazz up fish. Well, this little twist will make the family anxious to get to the table!

- 6 catfish fillets, fresh or frozen
- 1 cup finely crushed cheese crackers
- ¼ cup sesame seed
- 1 tablespoon chopped fresh parsley
- ½ teaspoon salt
- ¼ teaspoon black pepper
- ¼ teaspoon cayenne pepper
- ½ cup (1 stick) butter or margarine, melted
- Grated Parmesan cheese (optional)

Thaw fish fillets if frozen. Preheat oven to 400°F. In a shallow bowl, combine cracker crumbs, sesame seed, parsley, salt, and black and cayenne peppers. Dip fish fillets in melted butter, then roll fillets in cracker-crumb mixture. Place fillets in a single layer in a baking dish that has been coated with nonstick vegetable spray and bake for 15 to 20 minutes, until golden. Serve topped with Parmesan cheese, if desired.

Key West Fillets

about 4 servings

H*ere's something that'll perk up their tastebuds and have them clamoring for more, because this is how tastily they enjoy it in the Keys!*

- 1/4 cup (1/2 stick) butter or margarine
- 2/3 cup crushed saltine crackers
- 1/4 cup grated Parmesan cheese
- 1 teaspoon Italian seasoning
- 1/2 teaspoon salt
- 1/4 teaspoon garlic powder
- 1 pound fish fillets
- Juice of 1/2 lime

Preheat oven to 350°F. Melt butter in a 9" × 13" baking pan in the oven. Meanwhile, in a shallow dish, combine cracker crumbs, Parmesan cheese, Italian seasoning, salt, and garlic powder. Dip fillets in melted butter, then in cracker-crumb mixture. Arrange fish in a single layer in the baking pan, sprinkle with lime juice, and bake for about 20 minutes, until fish is tender and flakes easily with a fork.

NOTE: In Key West, the fish fillets would naturally be grouper, but any fish fillets will work—white or pink or dark. Try sole, flounder, or whatever you like best. Do your own thing 'cause whatever's on sale will work fine.

Grilled Fish

3 to 4 servings

I*f you've been looking for easy fish–this is it! Try it on the barbecue. (And hinged grill baskets make it even easier!)*

- 1½ pounds white-fleshed fish fillets (cod, haddock, or sole)
- ½ cup Italian salad dressing

In a large bowl, marinate fillets in salad dressing in refrigerator for 20 to 30 minutes. Preheat barbecue grill. Place marinated fillets in a hinged grill basket that's been coated with nonstick vegetable spray. Grill for about 10 minutes per inch-thickness of fish or until fish flakes easily with a fork.

NOTE: Before grilling, try sprinkling fish with Parmesan cheese. I prefer Italian dressing for the marinade, but just about any dressing will work. And it can have campfire taste even without any seasonings–mesquite and hickory-flavored charcoals, wood chips, and lava rocks have built-in flavor . . . with no mess! If you'd like to make this indoors, preheat your broiler and brush the broiler pan or baking dish with oil. Place the fish about 4 inches from the broiler unit and broil for about 10 minutes per inch-thickness of fish.

Stuffed Sole Fillets

8 servings

This is a nice change from the regular bread-type stuffings because the potatoes are so light. Nice for company, too; the fish looks so fancy all rolled up.

About 2½ cups mashed potatoes
1 teaspoon dried dillweed
½ teaspoon salt
8 sole fillets (3 to 4 ounces each)
⅓ cup butter, melted
Chopped fresh parsley for garnish

Preheat oven to 375°F. In a large bowl, thoroughly blend the potatoes with the dillweed and salt. Spread about ¼ cup potato mixture on each fillet. Roll fillets and place, seam-side down, in a 7″ × 11″ baking pan that has been coated with nonstick vegetable spray. Brush melted butter over fillet rolls and bake for 20 to 25 minutes or until fish flakes easily with a fork. Sprinkle with chopped parsley.

NOTE: You can substitute instant mashed potatoes for fresh. I often like to add ½ teaspoon each of garlic powder and thyme in place of the salt.

Potatoes and Rice

Potatoes and rice are easy and always available. That must be why they're food staples throughout the world. They can be used as thickeners, side dishes, desserts . . . and on and on.

My Mama had eight or ten ways to make them. She didn't have time to be much more creative, so we enjoyed those same ones over and over. Well, it seems that it was the same in every family, so that gave me lots of choices for special potato and rice dishes! A few of the MR. FOOD® TV show favorites are here. They were somebody's family favorites. So, enjoy . . . and feel at home.

Easy French-Fancy Rice

4 to 6 servings

Making holiday-special meals means exotic, intricate recipes—right? Not with this one. It's so easy . . . serve it anytime, and it'll make any meal holiday-special and gourmet-tasting special. (Thanks, Pat.)

- 1 large onion, diced
- 2 tablespoons (¼ stick) butter or margarine
- 2 cups cooked rice
- 2 eggs, beaten
- 1 cup milk
- 1 cup (4 ounces) shredded Swiss cheese
- ¼ teaspoon salt
- Pepper to taste

Preheat oven to 375°F. In a large skillet, sauté the onion in the butter until golden. In a large bowl, mix the sautéed onion with the remaining ingredients. Pour the mixture into a greased 1½-quart baking dish and bake for 20 to 25 minutes or until lightly golden and heated through.

NOTE: Garnish with chopped parsley and paprika.

Mama's Harvest Pudding

4 to 6 servings

Mama's cooking—you can almost taste it just thinking about it! What she could do with harvest items was mouth-watering. Well, we can have that same yesterday-taste but with today-easy. Wouldn't Mama be proud of us?

- 1 cup peeled and grated sweet potato (about 1 medium or ½ pound)
- 1 cup peeled and grated carrot (about 3 carrots)
- 1 cup peeled, cored, and grated apple (about 1 large apple)
- ½ cup sugar
- ½ cup raisins
- ½ cup cracker crumbs or cracker meal
- ½ cup chopped prunes
- 2 tablespoons lemon juice
- ½ teaspoon ground cinnamon
- ½ teaspoon salt
- ½ cup (1 stick) butter or margarine, melted

Preheat oven to 350°F. In a large bowl, combine all ingredients; mix well. Pour mixture into a greased 8″ × 4″ loaf pan and bake for 45 minutes or until heated through. Serve warm as a side dish.

NOTE: A food processor makes grating a snap. Your loaf pan doesn't have to be the same size I use. Any one close to that size will do.

Three-Cheese Potatoes

6 servings

E*verybody loves potatoes, but sometimes we'd like to have them a little different. Here's a way to prepare them that can turn a simple meal into a feast!*

- 6 medium-sized potatoes, peeled
- 1½ cups cottage cheese, dry curd or pot style (1 16-ounce container is about 1⅔ cups)
- 1 cup sour cream
- 2 tablespoons chopped scallions
- 2 tablespoons chopped fresh parsley
- 2 teaspoons dried dillweed
- 1½ teaspoons salt
- ½ cup (2 ounces) shredded Cheddar cheese
- ½ cup (2 ounces) shredded Monterey Jack cheese

Place the potatoes in a large pot, add enough salted water to cover, and bring to a boil; cook until just done, about 15 to 20 minutes. Preheat oven to 350°F. Drain potatoes, cool slightly, then cut into ¼-inch slices; place slices in a large bowl. In a separate bowl, combine cottage cheese, sour cream, scallions, parsley, dillweed, and salt; add to potatoes and mix gently. Spoon mixture into a lightly greased 1½-quart casserole dish; sprinkle Cheddar and Monterey Jack cheeses over the top. Bake for about 30 minutes or until light golden and bubbly.

NOTE: If dry curd or pot style cottage cheese is not available, use small curd cottage cheese but strain it first. You can make this dish lighter by using low-fat cheeses and sour cream, and you can cut down on the salt, if you prefer.

Potato Magics

24 large or 72 small puffs

We all love those old-fashioned tastes, but the old-fashioned hard work? No, thanks! Here's a shortcut way to have a taste of the good old days—you know, when they called these dumplings or knishes or baked pirogi or just potato puffs. This quick way they form their own crust. It's a super appetizer when made in a smaller size, too.

- 3 pounds potatoes, peeled and quartered
- 3 tablespoons olive oil
- 1 cup chopped onion
- 1 cup cracker or bread crumbs
- 2 teaspoons salt
- ½ teaspoon pepper
- 2 eggs yolks, beaten

Place the potatoes in a large pot, add enough salted water to cover, and bring to a boil. Reduce heat and simmer over medium heat for 25 to 30 minutes, or until potatoes are tender. Drain water; mash potatoes and allow to cool. Preheat oven to 400°F. In a skillet, heat the olive oil; sauté onion until tender. Add onion, cracker crumbs, salt, and pepper to potatoes; remash them. Coat cookie sheets with nonstick vegetable spray. Roll potato mixture into balls with your hands and place the balls on the cookie sheets; brush them with egg yolk. Bake for about 45 minutes, until crusty golden brown.

NOTE: Serve as an hors d'oeuvre, side dish, or snack, or even for brunch.

Spanish Rice

6 servings

H*ere's an all-time favorite that can be a side dish or a whole meal. It's quick and easy and made all in one pan. OLÉ!*

- 2 tablespoons vegetable oil
- 1 pound lean ground beef
- 1 cup chopped onion
- 1 cup chopped green bell pepper
- 1 cup uncooked rice
- 2 teaspoons chili powder
- 1½ cups water
- 1 teaspoon seasoned salt
- ½ teaspoon ground cumin
- ½ teaspoon ground black pepper
- 1 can (8 ounces) tomato sauce
- 1 can (14½ ounces) whole tomatoes, drained and chopped

In a large skillet, heat the oil over medium heat. Add the beef, onion, and green pepper, cooking until the meat is browned; drain liquid. Stir in remaining ingredients; reduce heat, cover, and simmer for 20 minutes or until rice is tender.

NOTE: For a lighter touch, you can substitute ground turkey or veal for the beef.

Lemon Rice

4 to 6 servings

***H**ow about a light and easy side dish to accompany tonight's supper? It's the perfect "go-along" for everything from chicken to ribs.*

- 1 cup uncooked white rice
- 2 tablespoons butter or margarine
- 2 garlic cloves, minced
- 1 teaspoon grated lemon peel
- ¼ teaspoon pepper
- 2 cups chicken broth
- 2 tablespoons chopped fresh parsley

In a large saucepan, combine all ingredients, except parsley; bring mixture to a boil, stirring once or twice. Lower heat, cover tightly, and simmer for 15 minutes or until liquid is absorbed. (Cook brown rice for about 45 minutes; parboiled rice for about 20 minutes.) Stir in parsley and serve.

NOTE: Serve with your favorite meat, chicken, or fish. For flavor variations, try adding a spice, some chopped green bell pepper, or a few chopped walnuts. Whatever touches you give it will work to make it "your very own."

Mashed Potato Pancakes

about 24 small pancakes

H*ow about a quick and easy way to bring a smile to your face and theirs? Did I say easy? I meant extra-easy!! These aren't exactly like the original grated raw potato pancakes, but we don't get grated knuckles, either.*

4 cups water
1 stick (½ cup) butter or margarine
2 teaspoons salt
4 cups instant potato flakes
1¼ cups milk
1 large onion, diced
¼ cup chopped fresh parsley
1 cup all-purpose flour
3 eggs, beaten
Vegetable oil for frying (½ inch deep in large skillet)

In a large saucepan, combine water, butter, and salt; bring to a boil. Remove from heat, add potato flakes, and mix. Add milk, then mix again until smooth; let cool. Add onion, parsley, flour, and eggs; mix. In a large skillet, heat oil; using about ¼ cup of mixture per pancake, form pancakes and fry in skillet for 2 minutes on each side, until golden. Drain pancakes on paper towels.

NOTE: Serve with applesauce, sour cream, ketchup, or syrup—whatever's your favorite.

Quick Italian Rice

6 servings

In the mood for a traditional Italian dish that cooks up creamy rich, but without all the work? Try this! We might have heard this referred to as risotto . . . whatever it's called, it's still easy.

- 1 cup medium-grain uncooked rice
- 2 cups chicken broth, divided
- 1 tablespoon butter or margarine
- ½ cup thinly sliced carrots
- ½ cup thinly sliced zucchini
- ½ cup thinly sliced yellow squash
- ¼ cup dry white wine
- ¼ cup grated Parmesan cheese
- ¼ teaspoon white pepper

In a large saucepan, combine the rice and 1½ cups of the chicken broth; bring to a boil, stirring occasionally, then lower heat to simmer. Cover and cook for about 15 minutes; set aside. In a large skillet, cook carrots, zucchini, and yellow squash in butter just until softened, about 2 to 3 minutes. Add wine and cook for 2 minutes more; set aside and keep warm. Add remaining ½ cup broth to hot rice over medium-high heat, stirring until broth is absorbed. Stir in cooked vegetables, cheese, and pepper. Serve immediately.

French Roasted Potatoes

12 servings

T*urn any meal into a feast by making the potatoes special. Sounds difficult, doesn't it? Well, it's not. But it is that special!!*

- 24 small red-skinned potatoes, quartered
- 4 garlic cloves, coarsely chopped
- ⅔ cup Dijon mustard
- 1 stick (½ cup) butter or margarine, melted
- ¼ cup chopped fresh parsley

Preheat oven to 350°F. Place the potatoes and garlic in a lightly greased roasting pan; cover tightly with foil. Bake for 60 minutes or until potatoes are just fork-tender. In a medium-sized bowl, blend mustard, butter, and parsley; toss with hot potatoes. Bake, uncovered, for 15 minutes more. Serve immediately.

Armenian Holiday Pilaf

10 cups

Thought you could get this only in a restaurant or at an Armenian holiday table? Wait'll you see how easy and tasty this side dish can be. And it'll feed a whole gang! (The wide noodles are the "little bit different" here.) Amazing!! So much taste in so few ingredients.

- ½ pound uncooked wide egg noodles
- 1 stick (½ cup) butter or margarine
- 3 cans (10½ ounces each) chicken broth
- 2 cups uncooked rice (*not* instant rice)

In a large saucepan, brown the noodles in the butter. Add broth and rice and bring to a full boil. Lower heat and simmer, covered, for 20 minutes.

NOTE: This is the greatest addition to any dinner—chicken, beef, turkey, anything!

Vermont Maple-Glazed Sweet Potatoes

5 servings

W*e can put a taste of New England on our dinner tables, then sit back and watch for the smiles.*

- 5 sweet potatoes, peeled and cut into quarters or sixths
- 4 tablespoons (½ stick) butter or margarine, melted
- ¼ cup granulated sugar
- ¼ cup firmly packed brown sugar
- ½ cup maple syrup
- ½ teaspoon salt
- ¼ teaspoon white pepper
- ½ teaspoon ground cinnamon
- ¼ teaspoon nutmeg

Preheat oven to 350°F. Place potatoes in a 9″ × 13″ baking dish. In a bowl, mix together remaining ingredients; toss with potatoes to coat well. Bake, uncovered, for 1 hour. Stir and continue baking for ½ hour more, until glazed. Stir when removed from oven, then serve.

NOTE: If you don't have real Vermont maple syrup, you can use maple-flavored pancake syrup. But boy, oh boy, there's nothing in the world like real maple syrup.

Hash Brown Potatoes

8 to 10 servings

These are a favorite side dish with any meal, and now you can make them crispy and delicious right in your own kitchen! We can sure remember the old neighborhood with this one.

- 1 package (2 pounds) frozen hash brown potatoes, thawed
- ¼ cup chopped onion
- 1 can (10¾ ounces) cream of chicken or mushroom soup
- 1 container (16 ounces) sour cream
- 2 cups (8 ounces) shredded Cheddar cheese
- 1 teaspoon salt
- ¼ teaspoon black pepper
- 1 green bell pepper, chopped

TOPPING

- 1 cup dry bread crumbs
- ½ cup (1 stick) margarine, melted

Preheat oven to 350°F. In a large bowl, mix together the hash brown potatoes, onion, soup, sour cream, Cheddar cheese, salt, black pepper, and green pepper. Spread potato mixture in a greased 9″ × 13″ baking pan. Mix together topping ingredients and spread over potato mixture. Bake for 45 minutes to 1 hour, until golden brown.

Company Potatoes

12 servings

W*e have potatoes so often that we sometimes think we need something more special for company. Well, potatoes can be made special and simple and rich-tasting, like this dish!*

- 4 to 5 large baking potatoes, peeled and coarsely grated
- 2 cups (8 ounces) grated Cheddar cheese
- 2 tablespoons chopped fresh parsley
- 2 tablespoons chopped scallions
- 1/4 teaspoon salt
- 1/4 teaspoon pepper
- 1 cup half-and-half
- 2 cups (8 ounces) grated Swiss cheese
- Paprika for garnish

Preheat oven to 500°F. In a large bowl, combine all ingredients, except Swiss cheese and paprika. Coat a 12″ × 14″ baking dish or two 7″ × 11″ baking dishes with nonstick vegetable spray; put potato mixture in baking dish(es). Sprinkle with Swiss cheese and paprika, then bake for 45 minutes or until golden brown and crisp. Serve hot.

Cajun Rice

about 8 cups

Cajun food is all the rage 'cause it sounds so "in" and tastes so down-home good!! Try this with any meal at all and the whole meal becomes "in." Well, of course it's simple–just look at it.

- 2 tablespoons vegetable oil
- ½ pound chicken livers
- 2 teaspoons salt, divided
- 4 tablespoons (½ stick) margarine
- 1 cup diced onion
- ½ green or red bell pepper, diced
- ¼ pound (4 ounces) diced mushrooms
- ½ pound diced cooked sausage (like kielbasa)
- 1 tablespoon Worcestershire sauce
- ½ teaspoon garlic powder
- ½ teaspoon hot pepper sauce
- 6 tablespoons chopped fresh parsley
- 1 teaspoon black pepper
- 6 cups cooked rice

In a large skillet, heat oil; sauté chicken livers with ½ teaspoon of the salt until done (no pink should remain). Dice the cooked chicken livers and set aside. In the same skillet, sauté onion, bell pepper, and mushrooms in the margarine until soft. Add diced chicken livers and sausage. Add remaining ingredients to skillet and cook until warmed through.

French Fry Crispy

6 to 8 servings

If you love French fries (and who doesn't!), here's a shortcut way of making them, starting with frozen fries. Know how much labor that saves us to begin with? And watch, they'll fight for the crisp part.

- 1 bag (24 ounces) frozen deep-fry French fries
- 1 cup (4 ounces) grated sharp Cheddar cheese
- 2 tablespoons chopped fresh parsley
- ½ cup half-and-half
- 1½ teaspoons salt
- Dash of pepper

Preheat oven to 450°F. Spread the French fries in a 9″ × 13″ baking dish. Sprinkle with cheese, parsley, half-and-half, salt, and pepper. Cover and bake for 1 hour or until bubbly and done.

NOTE: I sometimes leave them in a little longer because I like them nice and brown.

Fast Fried Rice

6 to 8 servings

Now you can make one of everybody's favorite "Chinese restaurant" dishes in your own kitchen–and it's such a snap!

- 4 to 5 tablespoons vegetable oil
- 1 bunch scallions, sliced on an angle, about ¼ inch thick
- 2 teaspoons curry powder
- ¼ teaspoon garlic powder
- 2 teaspoons salt
- 8 cups cooked rice

In a large saucepan, heat oil; sauté scallions quickly, just until warm. Stir in the remaining ingredients; continue cooking just until heated through.

NOTE: For color and flavor variety you can add chopped cooked scrambled egg, diced cooked green pepper or broccoli stems, or diced cooked chicken or ham. Enjoy it your own way!

Garlic Roasted Potatoes

6 to 8 servings

These are one better than just regular baked potatoes because they are more homemade tasting!

- 2½ to 3 pounds small potatoes, rinsed and quartered (skins on)
- ¼ cup olive oil
- 1 head garlic, sliced in half crosswise and separated
- ½ teaspoon salt
- ½ teaspoon pepper

Preheat oven to 450°F. Place potatoes in a 9″ × 13″ baking dish. Cover the potatoes with the oil, garlic, salt, and pepper; mix to coat potatoes. Bake for 50 to 60 minutes, turning occasionally, until golden brown. Discard garlic before serving.

NOTE: This works just as well with regular-sized potatoes as it does with the little creamer type. Just cut them into large chunks.

Lyonnaise Potatoes

about 4 servings

H*ere's that "everybody's family favorite"–potatoes and onions together. Mama had to play referee in our house 'cause we'd fight to get the crispy ones!*

- 1/4 cup vegetable oil
- 1 large onion, chopped
- 1 1/2 pounds boiled peeled potatoes, cooled and cut into thick slices
- 1/4 cup chopped fresh parsley
- 1/2 teaspoon salt
- 1/2 teaspoon pepper

In a large nonstick skillet, heat the oil. Add the onion and potatoes and sauté over medium heat for about 20 to 25 minutes or until golden brown. Remove from heat and add parsley, salt, and pepper; mix well. Serve immediately.

NOTE: These potatoes are so versatile that they can be served with anything from Chicken Kiev to a hamburger to an omelet!

Pasta

Whether it's called pasta or noodles or crisp-fry or whatever, it's what Mama would serve in some shape or form at most every meal. That's because it was an inexpensive way to fill up our plates and our appetites.

And, is it easy! Just boil it and that's it. It goes with everything, too. It's only recently that we found out about pasta being such a great energy food. Even more reason to be creative in finding new ways to enjoy it.

Try it in any form you want. Develop your own favorites. It easily becomes every country, region, neighborhood, and family. There are no rules, except that every time you have pasta you'll hear lots of OOH it's so GOOD!!™

Pasta Pedro

8 servings

This is like a Tex-Mex version of Fettuccine Alfredo, but it's faster and easier and more exciting and no-fail! It takes only minutes, so I'm always ready for whoever and whatever.

1 pound uncooked fettuccine noodles
6 tablespoons margarine
⅔ cup picante sauce
⅔ cup grated Parmesan cheese
1 cup sour cream
¼ teaspoon salt
Chopped fresh parsley for garnish

In a large pot of boiling water, cook noodles until tender; drain and set aside in a large bowl (keep noodles warm). Meanwhile, in a saucepan, combine margarine, picante sauce, and Parmesan cheese; cook over low heat, stirring, until margarine melts. Remove from heat; stir in sour cream and salt. Pour picante sauce mixture over warm fettuccine noodles and toss. Sprinkle with parsley and serve.

NOTE: Any kind of pasta will work. You can also add broccoli or cooked chopped chicken or pepperoni for a whole-meal treat.

Better Baked Ziti

about 8 servings

Sounds like it's old-fashioned difficult but it's really one of the easiest (and least expensive) ways to feed a whole gang. They'll love it this way 'cause for some reason this one seems richer and smoother than the regular ones. And look, five simple ingredients!

- ½ pound ziti
- 1 container (15 ounces) ricotta cheese
- 3 cups (12 ounces) shredded mozzarella cheese, divided
- 3 cups bottled spaghetti sauce, divided
- ½ cup grated Parmesan cheese

Preheat oven to 350°F. In a large pot, cook ziti in boiling water until just barely tender; drain and place in a large bowl. Mix the ricotta cheese and half the mozzarella cheese with the ziti. Grease a 9″ × 13″ baking pan; cover bottom of pan with half the spaghetti sauce. Spoon the ziti mixture into the pan; cover with the remaining spaghetti sauce. Sprinkle with the Parmesan cheese and top with the remaining mozzarella cheese. Bake for 20 to 30 minutes or until cheese melts and is lightly golden.

NOTE: I especially like the new hearty-style prepared spaghetti sauces with this and when I don't have ziti-shaped pasta on hand, I simply substitute other shapes.

Quick Homemade Macaroni and Cheese

4 servings

Today most of us think macaroni and cheese only comes in all-in-one boxes, but we can sometimes make it better with what's right in the house. It's just as easy and yet so much more homey than the boxed versions.

- ½ pound elbow macaroni
- ½ cup milk
- 1 cup (about ½ pound) diced Cheddar cheese or cubed processed cheese spread (like Velveeta®)
- ¼ teaspoon dry mustard
- ¼ teaspoon salt
- Dried basil, oregano, or chili powder to taste (optional)

In a large pot of boiling water, cook macaroni until just tender. Meanwhile, in a small saucepan, heat milk and cheese together over medium heat until cheese melts; add remaining ingredients. Drain macaroni, then place it in a deep bowl. Toss the macaroni with the cheese mixture and serve.

NOTE: You can use a flavored cheese or even add a sprinkle of your own favorite spice. For a heartier dish, you can add some diced bologna or pepperoni.

Ziti with Broccoli

about 8 servings

Pasta is really popular these days and so is old-fashioned, down-home taste. Well, here's a simple restaurant version that has it all!

- 1 pound ziti
- 2 tablespoons olive oil
- 2 garlic cloves, crushed
- 2 packages (10 ounces each) frozen chopped broccoli, thawed and well drained
- 1 cup grated Parmesan cheese
- 4 cups heavy cream
- 2 cups (8 ounces) shredded mozzarella cheese

Preheat oven to 350°F. In a large pot of boiling water, cook ziti until just barely tender; drain pasta, place in a large bowl, and set aside. In a skillet, heat the olive oil over medium heat and sauté garlic until lightly browned, about 1 minute. Combine garlic, broccoli, Parmesan cheese, and heavy cream with ziti; spoon mixture into a large baking dish. Top with mozzarella cheese and bake, covered, for 20 to 30 minutes or until heated through.

NOTE: You can cut the "heavy" of the cream by substituting 4 cups half-and-half or 2 cups cream with 2 cups milk for the 4 cups heavy cream.

Reuben Macaroni Salad

about 6 servings

These days, salads are more popular than ever before. And the right salad can be the whole meal–while it gets us out of the kitchen fast. Not a bad idea, eh? Especially when the salad tastes like a six-course meal, just like a Reuben sandwich does!

- 1½ cups elbow, ditalini, or twist macaroni
- ½ pound cooked corned beef, diced
- 1 cup (4 ounces) shredded Swiss cheese
- 1 can (16 ounces) sauerkraut, drained
- ½ teaspoon caraway seed
- ⅔ cup bottled Russian dressing
- 2 tomatoes, cut into wedges for garnish (optional)

In a large pot of boiling water, cook macaroni until tender; drain and cool. In a large bowl, combine the corned beef, cheese, sauerkraut, caraway seed, and Russian dressing. Add cooked macaroni and toss thoroughly. Serve with tomato wedges, if desired.

NOTE: If you don't like sauerkraut, drained coleslaw works just as well. Also, you can make your own Russian dressing by mixing ½ cup mayonnaise with 3 tablespoons ketchup.

Creamy Italian Pasta Salad

3 cups

This pasta salad is just the thing for a cheery side dish or a light main dish.

- 1½ cups uncooked twist pasta
- 1 cup mayonnaise
- 2 tablespoons red wine vinegar
- 1 garlic clove, minced
- 1 tablespoon chopped fresh basil or 1 to 2 teaspoons dried basil
- 1 teaspoon salt
- ¼ teaspoon black pepper
- 1 cup quartered cherry tomatoes
- ½ cup coarsely chopped green bell pepper
- ½ cup chopped ripe olives

In a large pot of boiling water, cook pasta until tender; rinse with cold water and drain. Meanwhile, in a large bowl, combine mayonnaise, vinegar, garlic, basil, salt, and black pepper. Add pasta, cherry tomatoes, green pepper, and olives; toss to coat well. Cover and refrigerate until ready to use. Serve chilled.

NOTE: Feel free to add other colorful veggies, like cut-up carrots or red onion or whatever you have on hand.

Noodles Pennsylvania Dutch Kluski

8 to 10 servings

This is one of those dishes that brings you back to the good old days from the very first taste–but it's today-easy to make! That's probably why my cousin still makes it as a side dish once a week. (And the family looks forward to it.)

- 1 pound egg noodles
- 2 packages (10 ounces each) frozen chopped spinach, thawed and well drained
- 1 stick (½ cup) margarine, melted
- 1½ cups milk
- 3 eggs, beaten
- 2 packages (1 2-ounce box) onion soup mix
- ½ cup grated Parmesan cheese

Preheat oven to 350°F. In a large pot of boiling water, cook noodles until tender; drain. In a large bowl, mix all ingredients together. Coat a 9" × 13" baking dish with nonstick vegetable spray; place noodle mixture in baking dish and cover tightly. Bake for 40 to 45 minutes or until slightly golden around the edges.

Cheesy Noodles Italian Style

6 appetizer or 4 main-dish servings

What's easy, inexpensive, and delicious? If you guessed Cheesy Noodles Italian Style, you guessed right! And here's the way.

- 1 pound pasta or egg noodles
- 4 tablespoons (½ stick) butter or margarine
- ¼ cup olive oil
- 1 cup finely chopped fresh basil
- 4 garlic cloves, finely chopped
- ¾ cup grated Romano or Parmesan cheese
- ½ teaspoon salt
- ½ teaspoon black pepper
- ¼ teaspoon dried oregano
- ¼ teaspoon crushed red pepper

In a large pot of boiling water, cook pasta just until tender. Drain, place in a large bowl, and set aside (keep warm). In a skillet, heat the butter and olive oil; add the basil and garlic and sauté for 1 to 2 minutes. Add the basil and garlic mixture and remaining ingredients to the pasta and mix. Serve hot.

NOTE: Some French or Italian bread would go great with this dish. Just think of the dunking possibilities!

Seashore Fettuccine

3 to 4 servings

The greatest part about this dish is that you can use whatever seafood is brought home–whether it was caught or bought. And it makes you feel like it's summertime at the beach. Summer or not–enjoy!

- 1 pound fettuccine noodles
- 1 stick (½ cup) butter or margarine
- 1 small onion, diced
- 12 ounces fresh or frozen, whole or broken shrimp, thawed
- ¼ teaspoon dried basil
- ⅛ teaspoon crushed red pepper
- ½ teaspoon salt
- Pinch black pepper
- 1 can (8 ounces) tomato sauce
- 1 container (8 ounces) heavy cream
- ½ cup grated Parmesan cheese

In a large pot of boiling water, cook pasta until tender; drain, place in a large bowl, and set aside. In a large skillet, melt butter; add onion, shrimp, basil, red pepper, salt, and black pepper. Sauté for about 2 minutes, then add the tomato sauce and heavy cream. Bring to a boil. Simmer until sauce is creamy, about 3 minutes. Add sauce and Parmesan cheese to pasta; mix and serve.

NOTE: This also tastes great with imitation crabmeat or scallops.

Garden Pasta

3 to 4 servings

Everybody likes pasta–pasta for lunch, pasta for dinner. It's popular because it's delicious and it goes with anything, anytime. This is a real 90's dish that takes just minutes to prepare–but it still has all of Mama's old-time long-cooked tastes.

- 1 jar (6 ounces) marinated artichoke hearts, undrained
- ½ cup finely chopped onion
- 1 garlic clove, finely chopped, or ½ teaspoon bottled chopped garlic
- 2 cups diced fresh tomatoes
- ½ teaspoon Italian seasoning
- ½ teaspoon salt
- ½ teaspoon dried basil
- ½ pound egg or spinach noodles or linguine
- ⅓ cup grated Parmesan cheese
- 4 tablespoons (¼ cup) butter or margarine, softened

Drain liquid from artichoke hearts into a large skillet. Cut larger artichoke hearts in half and set aside. Add onion and garlic to skillet; simmer over a low heat until softened. Add tomatoes, Italian seasoning, salt, and basil; cover and simmer for 10 minutes. Uncover and continue cooking until sauce thickens slightly, about 10 minutes more. Add artichokes and simmer for a few minutes longer. Meanwhile, in a large pot of boiling water, cook noodles just until tender; drain and toss with Parmesan cheese and softened butter. Serve pasta with the artichoke sauce.

NOTE: Before serving, sprinkle with extra Parmesan cheese, if desired. For a fresh garden flavor, try adding some shredded zucchini or fresh scallions.

Easy Pasta with Veggies

about 6 side-dish servings

We've become so used to fresh and frozen vegetables that we've almost forgotten how handy and down-home tasting canned veggies can be. After all, most of us grew up with canned vegetables 'cause Mama used a lot of them. Today, canned veggies are better than ever—less salty, crisper, fresher tasting, plus there are more varieties. This easy recipe gives us that "yesterday" taste better than ever. And it's still mostly "right off the shelf."

- 12 ounces (3/4 pound) twist pasta (about 6 cups uncooked)
- 1/4 cup olive oil
- 1 large red bell pepper, seeded, halved lengthwise, and cut into thin strips
- 2 teaspoons minced garlic
- 1 can (16 ounces) mixed vegetables, drained
- 2 tablespoons dried basil
- 1/4 teaspoon salt
- 1/4 teaspoon black pepper
- 1/2 cup grated Parmesan cheese

In a large pot of boiling water, cook pasta until tender; drain and return to pot to keep warm. Meanwhile, in a large skillet, heat olive oil until moderately hot; add the red pepper and garlic and sauté for 2 minutes, or until crisp-tender. Stir in the drained mixed vegetables, basil, salt, and black pepper; cook for 2 minutes more to heat through. In a large bowl, toss vegetable mixture with pasta and Parmesan cheese and mix well.

NOTE: You can use thawed frozen veggies if you like, but canned is sometimes easier, handier, and quicker.

Orzo Casserole

about 10 servings

This is a casserole that's the perfect go-along to any picnic or party because it goes along with whatever we're serving it with. And, to start with, everybody loves pasta, so we automatically win.

- 2 tablespoons butter or margarine
- 1 garlic clove, minced, or ½ teaspoon bottled garlic
- 1½ cups orzo or Rosa Marina pasta
- 1 envelope (1 ounce) onion soup mix
- 3¼ cups water
- 1 package (12 ounces) mushrooms, sliced (about 4 cups)
- ¼ cup chopped fresh parsley

In a large saucepan, melt butter over medium heat; add garlic and pasta and cook, stirring constantly, for about 2½ minutes or until golden. In a large bowl, combine onion soup mix with water; add to pasta mixture. Bring to a boil, then reduce heat and simmer, covered, for 10 minutes. Add mushrooms (do not stir); simmer, covered, for 10 minutes more. Stir in parsley. Place mixture in a serving bowl or casserole dish and let stand for 10 minutes or until liquid is absorbed. Serve.

Sesame Noodles

3 to 4 servings

Ya know those Oriental noodles that are served as a side dish in Chinese restaurants? Everybody wants to make them at home. Well, you can, easily! And get ready to hear a lot of cheers when you serve them!

1 pound pasta (your favorite type)
1 box (6 ounces) frozen pea pods, thawed
2 red bell peppers, diced
1 cucumber, peeled, seeded, and diced
6 scallions, chopped

SESAME DRESSING

¼ cup sesame oil
½ cup peanut or vegetable oil
¼ cup soy sauce
2 tablespoons lemon juice
½ teaspoon ground ginger
2 garlic cloves
6 scallions, chopped
¾ cup chunky peanut butter

In a large pot of boiling water, cook pasta until tender; cool under running water and drain. Meanwhile, thoroughly blend all Sesame Dressing ingredients in a blender or food processor. Toss pasta with pea pods, red peppers, cucumber, scallions, and about 1½ cups Sesame Dressing.

NOTE: Serve as a side dish or a salad. Topped with grilled chicken or steak, it's a perfect main course. If you make the Sesame Dressing in advance or want to save the extra, it will keep for up to a week in the refrigerator. The recipe will yield about 2 cups dressing.

Noodle Kugel (Pudding)

15 to 18 servings

This one will have you daydreaming about the good old days. You'll find yourself going back for seconds (and maybe even thirds!). This pudding was a standard in the old neighborhood, and everybody had their little secret touch with it. So, use yours, too. It all works!

- 1 pound egg noodles
- 2 tablespoons vegetable oil, divided
- 8 eggs, slightly beaten
- 1 container (16 ounces) cottage cheese
- 1 container (16 ounces) sour cream
- 1 can (20 ounces) crushed pineapple
- 1½ cups sugar
- Pinch of salt
- 2 teaspoons vanilla extract

Preheat oven to 350°F. To a large pot of boiling water, add 1 tablespoon oil and cook noodles until just tender, 5 to 7 minutes (do not overcook); drain and place in a large bowl. Add remaining oil to noodles, then add remaining ingredients and mix. Place noodle mixture in a 9″ × 13″ glass baking dish that has been coated with nonstick vegetable spray. Bake for 1¾ to 2 hours, uncovered, or until set and lightly browned and crisp.

NOTE: Vary the amounts of sugar, salt, and vanilla extract according to your own personal taste.

Plate of Pasta

3 to 4 servings

While rediscovering all those flavors of years ago, we've been finding out why Mama and Grandma made pasta so often—because it was so easy and delicious. (I'm sure that low cost had a lot to do with it, too.)

- ¼ cup olive oil
- 1 large onion, chopped
- 2 teaspoons minced garlic
- 1 box (10 ounces) frozen chopped broccoli, thawed
- 1 can (10½ ounces) chicken broth
- ½ cup chopped fresh parsley
- 1 teaspoon dried oregano
- 1 teaspoon dried basil
- ½ teaspoon salt
- ¼ teaspoon crushed red pepper
- 1 pound linguine or spaghetti

In a large pot of boiling water, cook pasta until tender. Meanwhile, in a large saucepan, heat olive oil; sauté onion and garlic until softened. Add broccoli, chicken broth, parsley, oregano, basil, salt, and red pepper. Simmer for 5 to 10 minutes and serve over pasta.

NOTE: If you want an instant white clam sauce, just add a can or two of chopped clams with the chicken broth. You can even add slices of cooked chicken or pepperoni for a new taste treat.

Roasted Peppers and Pasta

4 to 5 appetizer or 3 main-dish servings

Maybe we can't have summertime peppers all year at summertime prices, but we can have them at an affordable price if we buy them canned or jarred. Of course, they're not crunchy like fresh peppers, but they have a lot of good points and we can use them a lot of tasty ways. For instance, this is as homestyle-Italian as we could ever get.

- ½ pound linguine or spaghetti
- ¼ cup vegetable oil
- 4 garlic cloves, minced
- 4 jars (7¼ ounces each) roasted peppers, drained and coarsely chopped
- ¼ cup coarsely chopped pimiento-stuffed green olives
- 1 teaspoon dried basil
- 1 teaspoon salt
- 1 teaspoon dried oregano
- 1 teaspoon black pepper

In a large pot of boiling water, cook pasta until tender. In a large skillet, heat olive oil; sauté garlic just until soft. Add the remaining ingredients, except pasta, and stir-fry for about 10 minutes, until mixture is warmed through and well blended. Serve over pasta.

NOTE: Top with grated Parmesan cheese, if desired. For a different flavor, try adding a little cream or cooked sausage or anchovies or ricotta cheese, whatever you like!

Stuffed Shells

6 to 8 servings

There's nothing that gets the mouth watering more than a good old-fashioned Italian meal. Here's one that your family or company will applaud you for.

- 35 to 40 large pasta shells (12-ounce package) or 14 manicotti (8-ounce package) for stuffing
- 1 container (32 ounces) ricotta cheese
- 3 cups (12 ounces) shredded mozzarella cheese, divided
- ½ cup plus 2 tablespoons grated Parmesan or Romano cheese
- 2 eggs, beaten
- 1 tablespoon chopped fresh parsley
- 1 garlic clove, crushed
- 1 teaspoon salt
- ½ teaspoon pepper
- 3 cups spaghetti sauce, divided

Preheat oven to 350°F. In a large pot, bring salted water to a boil; add pasta. Return to a boil, then continue cooking for 5 to 6 minutes more, until pasta is just barely tender. Drain, cover with cold water, and drain again. In a large bowl, mix together the ricotta cheese, 2 cups of the mozzarella cheese, the ½ cup Parmesan cheese, eggs, parsley, garlic, salt, and pepper. Pour ½ cup spaghetti sauce onto bottom of each of 2 lightly greased 8-inch square glass baking dishes. Fill each shell or manicotti generously with cheese mixture, about 1 tablespoon in each shell. Place filled pasta in baking dishes. Pour 1 cup spaghetti sauce over each baking dish of pasta, then top each baking dish with ½ cup shredded mozzarella and 1 tablespoon Parmesan. Bake for 40 to 45 minutes, until lightly golden. Let set for 10 minutes before serving.

NOTE: An easy, efficient way to fill the pasta is to place the cheese mixture in a large resealable plastic storage bag with a corner snipped off; squeeze the filling into the pasta, using the storage bag like a pastry bag.

Tex-Mex Lasagna

about 6 servings

An all-time favorite Italian dish with a little twist of novelty can give us that great up-to-the-minute Tex-Mex flavor that everybody loves. With the fun and comfort of regular lasagna, this one's just as easy–maybe easier.

SAUCE

- 1 pound ground beef
- ½ cup chopped onion
- 1 cup tomato paste (1 6-ounce can contains about ⅔ cup)
- 1 cup picante sauce, medium or mild
- ¾ cup water
- 1 teaspoon dried oregano
- 1 teaspoon dried basil

- 1 cup ricotta or cottage cheese
- ¾ cup plus 1½ cups shredded mozzarella cheese
- ½ pound uncooked lasagna noodles

Make sauce by browning the beef with the onion in a large skillet; drain liquid. Add the tomato paste, picante sauce, water, oregano, and basil; mix well and set aside. In a large bowl, combine the ricotta cheese and the ¾ cup mozzarella cheese; set aside. Coat a 7″ × 11″ baking pan with nonstick vegetable spray. Layer ingredients in the pan, as follows: ⅓ cup sauce, half of the uncooked lasagna noodles and half the cheese mixture; repeat the same layers and top with the remaining sauce, then the 1½ cups mozzarella cheese. Cover and refrigerate overnight. The next day, bake in a preheated 350°F. oven for 1 hour or until light golden. Remove from oven and let stand for 20 minutes for easier serving.

Veggies

Remember Mama saying, "Eat your vegetables, they're good for you"? She must have known something! And lots of times she had to serve us veggies from a can. That was because we didn't have the growing and transportation systems we have now.

Then came frozen vegetables and we couldn't believe our good fortune! How lucky we were to be enjoying broccoli, cauliflower, corn, peas, and asparagus that were so close to fresh-from-the-garden. The same with cabbage, carrots, potatoes, and beets; they could now come from our freezers, ready to use, rather than shriveled from cold storage.

And today we can have all types of good-quality vegetables reasonably and abundantly all year 'round. The quality of canned and frozen vegetables is better than ever.

Sure, in-season fresh veggies will always be the most luscious and desirable, and no longer are we limited to only those grown in our own locality. Today our markets offer us California artichokes alongside Michigan potatoes, New York onions, Texas melons, and Florida limes and starfruit. WOW!! How our neighborhood has grown! That's a boon to our increasing interest in health, too.

Why, with today's veggies being easier, tastier, and more versatile than ever, Mama would surely say, "Eat *more* of your vegetables—they're *really* good for you!"

Vegetable Cheese Bake

about 12 servings

This is the perfect way to enjoy your veggies crunchy but still with those long-cooked-tasting juices. It's so cheesy-rich and mellow.

- ¼ cup vegetable oil
- 2 medium-sized baking potatoes, peeled and cubed
- 1 medium-sized zucchini, cut into ¼-inch slices (about 4 cups)
- 1 large onion, quartered and cut into ½-inch pieces
- 2 medium-sized green bell peppers, cut into ½-inch slices
- ½ pound mushrooms, cut into ½-inch slices (about 3½ cups)
- 3 garlic cloves, minced
- 4 cups (16 ounces) shredded mozzarella cheese for topping

SAUCE

- 1½ cups mild barbecue sauce
- ½ cup Burgundy wine
- ½ cup water
- 1 teaspoon dried thyme
- ¼ teaspoon black pepper

In a large skillet, heat oil until moderately hot; sauté potatoes, zucchini, onion, green peppers, mushrooms, and garlic for 3 to 5 minutes; set aside. In a large saucepan, combine all sauce ingredients and simmer for 10 minutes. Add sautéed vegetables to sauce and simmer for another 10 minutes; keep warm. Preheat oven to 350°F. Spoon vegetable/sauce mixture into a 9″ × 13″ glass baking dish and sprinkle with mozzarella cheese. Bake for 15 to 20 minutes or until cheese is bubbly and lightly golden.

Skillet Beans

8 servings

Want a veggie dish that tastes like a meal right from the chuck wagon? Here it is! It goes with any outdoor party or, come to think of it, any indoor party, also.

- 1 onion, thinly sliced
- 2 tablespoons butter
- 1 can (16 ounces) pork and beans or vegetarian beans
- 1 can (15 ounces) garbanzo beans, drained
- 2 packages (9 or 10 ounces) frozen green beans, thawed
- 3/4 cup bottled barbecue sauce
- 1 cup (4 ounces) shredded Cheddar cheese

In a large skillet, sauté onion in butter for about 5 minutes. Add pork and beans, garbanzo beans, green beans, and barbecue sauce; heat until bubbly, stirring occasionally. Sprinkle with cheese; heat until cheese melts.

NOTE: Sometimes I use white beans or black-eyed peas instead of the garbanzos. Add your own seasonings or even more veggies. It all works.

Noah's Squash

about 8 servings

W*hen zucchini and summer squash are bursting from our gardens all we have to do is "think 2." Use 2 of each here. Or make it anytime with 2 of your in-season favorites. (And it's so easy 'cause it all cooks together.)*

2 medium-sized zucchini, sliced
2 summer squash, sliced
2 medium-sized onions, peeled and sliced
2 tomatoes, quartered
2 garlic cloves, minced
2 tablespoons olive oil
½ cup green or black olives
½ teaspoon salt
¼ teaspoon pepper

In a large skillet or wok, combine all ingredients. Cook over medium heat, stirring occasionally, for about 20 minutes or until zucchini and summer squash are tender.

Crispy Onion Rings

6 to 8 servings

E*ver wonder how the restaurants make their onion rings so crispy-special? Now you can do it, too.*

- 3 or 4 Spanish-type onions
- 3 cups buttermilk or milk
- 1 cup all-purpose flour
- ⅔ cup water
- 1½ teaspoons baking powder
- 1 teaspoon salt
- 1 egg, beaten
- 1 tablespoon vegetable oil, plus extra for frying
- 1 teaspoon lemon juice
- ¼ teaspoon cayenne pepper

Peel onions and cut into ⅓-inch slices; separate into rings. Pour buttermilk into large shallow dish; add onion rings and soak for 30 minutes. In a large shallow dish, combine the flour, water, baking powder, salt, egg, the 1 tablespoon vegetable oil, lemon juice, and cayenne pepper; stir until smooth. In a skillet, heat oil for frying on medium-high heat. Remove onion rings from buttermilk and dip into flour mixture; place in skillet and fry in hot oil until golden brown. Drain onion rings on paper towels.

NOTE: If your onions are small, use 4. These rings come out crunchiest when made in an electric skillet, because it's easier to keep the oil at a consistent temperature.

Bell Pepper Hash

6 servings

When peppers are on sale, it makes this hash that much better! And it's perfect for adding that homemade touch to any meal.

- ½ cup chopped red bell pepper
- ½ cup chopped green bell pepper
- 1 cup crumbled fresh bread crumbs
- 1 cup (4 ounces) shredded Cheddar cheese
- ¾ cup milk
- 1 egg, beaten
- ¼ teaspoon salt
- ¼ teaspoon black pepper
- Butter or margarine

Preheat oven to 300°F. In a large bowl, combine all ingredients, except butter; pour mixture into a 1-quart baking dish. Dot with butter and bake for 45 minutes or until slightly brown and set.

NOTE: This is a great, easy side dish. For a lighter-style treat, you can use low-fat cheese, 2% milk, a lighter-type bread for bread crumbs, less salt, or even omit the egg yolk.

Broccoli Casserole

6 side-dish servings

Because it's so reasonable and versatile, here's another way to enjoy broccoli. And you've probably got all these ingredients on hand.

1 bunch broccoli, trimmed and cut into chunks
1 cup (4 ounces) grated Cheddar cheese
1 cup mayonnaise
1 can (10¾ ounces) cream of mushroom soup, undiluted
1 medium-sized onion, minced
2 eggs, well beaten
Seasoned bread crumbs

Preheat oven to 350°F. Boil or steam broccoli for 5 minutes. Meanwhile, in a large bowl, combine the Cheddar cheese, mayonnaise, mushroom soup, onion, and eggs; mix well. Add cooked broccoli to cheese mixture. Pour mixture into a greased 2-quart baking dish. Sprinkle top with bread crumbs and bake for 35 minutes or until lightly golden.

NOTE: You can use 2 packages (10 ounces each) frozen broccoli instead of fresh; just thaw it under cool water, drain it, and add to mixture (there's no need to cook it). You can add some chopped, cooked chicken or turkey to turn this side dish into a hearty main-course dish.

Veggies Roma

4 servings

H*aving a buffet party or need to prepare a dish to bring to one? This is your ticket to tons of raves.*

- ½ cup vegetable oil
- 1 eggplant, cut into 1-inch cubes (about 1½ pounds)
- 1 garlic clove, crushed
- ¼ cup tomato paste (a 6-ounce can contains about ⅔ cup)
- 1 can (14½ ounces) stewed or Italian tomatoes
- 2 cups waxed or green beans
- 1 teaspoon seasoned salt
- 1½ cups fresh bread crumbs
- ½ cup grated Parmesan cheese
- 1 package (6 ounces) mozzarella cheese, sliced

In a skillet, heat oil until moderately hot; sauté eggplant until browned, stirring occasionally. Add garlic, tomato paste, tomatoes, beans, and seasoned salt. Cover and simmer for 15 minutes. Preheat oven to 350°F. Pour half of vegetable mixture into a greased 1½-quart baking dish. Sprinkle with bread crumbs and Parmesan cheese. Cover with remaining vegetable mixture and top with mozzarella cheese slices. Bake for 30 minutes or until cheese melts and browns.

NOTE: Fresh, frozen, and canned beans all work well. If using fresh beans, be sure to cook them first. If using frozen beans, thaw them first. If using canned beans (16 ounces), be sure to drain them before adding to skillet. For a different taste treat, you can add a small chopped onion or other favorite veggies.

Summer Picnic Salad

3 to 4 servings

For that summertime taste anytime, try this colorful sparkler. Let's face it, cucumbers and tomatoes always say "summer."

- 2 cucumbers, sliced*
- 12 cherry tomatoes, halved
- ¼ cup mayonnaise
- ¼ cup sour cream
- 2 teaspoons dried oregano
- 1 teaspoon onion salt
- ½ teaspoon pepper
- ½ teaspoon garlic powder

In a large bowl, combine cucumber slices and tomatoes. In a small bowl, mix together the mayonnaise, sour cream, oregano, onion salt, pepper, and garlic powder; add mayonnaise mixture to vegetables and toss. Serve immediately—"fresh is best!"—or store in refrigerator for up to 2 days.

*NOTE: I like to leave some of the peel on the cucumbers for added color; I just wash them well, then remove strips of peel. You can remove the entire peel, if you prefer.

Garden Loaf

4 to 6 servings

Here's a way to turn your favorite veggie standards into a hearty main dish. It's an all-vegetable version of meat loaf. And it's so simple, you might wanna make two or three so you have them on hand, in the freezer.

- 1 cup finely chopped onion
- 1 cup finely chopped celery
- 1 cup shredded carrots
- 1/4 cup finely chopped green bell pepper
- 1 cup finely chopped walnuts
- 1 cup bread crumbs
- 1/2 teaspoon salt
- 1/2 teaspoon black pepper
- 1/2 teaspoon dried dillweed
- 1/2 cup mayonnaise
- 2 eggs, slightly beaten

Preheat oven to 350°F. Line an 8″ × 4″ loaf pan with foil; grease foil. In a large bowl, stir together onion, celery, carrots, green pepper, walnuts, bread crumbs, salt, black pepper, and dillweed. In a small bowl, stir together mayonnaise and eggs until smooth; stir mayonnaise mixture into vegetable mixture until well mixed. Pour mixture into prepared pan. Bake for 45 to 50 minutes or until lightly browned. Let cool in pan for about 15 minutes, then invert loaf and remove foil. Place right side up on serving platter and serve immediately or store in the refrigerator; reheat before serving.

Green Bean Bake

6 servings

Remember that favorite casserole from the '50s? Well, here it is, and after you taste it again you'll wonder why we ever took a vacation from this standby that was all the rage back then (and getting to be a rage again).

- ½ cup milk
- 1 can (10¾ ounces) condensed cream of mushroom soup
- 1 teaspoon soy sauce
- Dash of pepper
- 4 cups cut fresh green beans, cooked
- 1 can (2.8 ounces) French fried onions

Oven Method: Preheat oven to 350°F. Combine milk, soup, soy sauce, and pepper in a 1½-quart casserole dish. Stir in cooked green beans and half the French fried onions. Bake for 25 minutes or until hot; stir. Top with remaining French fried onions and bake for 5 minutes more.

Microwave Method: Combine milk, soup, soy sauce, and pepper in a 1½-quart microwaveable dish. Stir in cooked green beans and half the French fried onions. Cover with microwaveable lid; microwave on high for 7 minutes or until hot, stirring once during cooking. Top with remaining French fried onions and microwave on high, uncovered, for 1 minute more. Please remember that cooking times may vary slightly depending on the wattage of your microwave.

NOTE: Add cut-up chunks of cooked chicken or turkey and turn it into a whole meal. Instead of cooking fresh green beans, I sometimes use two 9-ounce packages frozen cut green beans or two 16-ounce cans cut green beans.

Broccoli Italiano

3 to 4 servings

Delicious with fresh or leftover broccoli, this can be a side dish or a main dish if served over pasta. And it's so quick and versatile! Yes, you're seeing right . . . just 3 ingredients!

- 1 bunch broccoli (about 1½ pounds), cut into spears
- ⅔ cup Italian salad dressing
- ⅓ cup dry white wine or water

In a large skillet, combine all ingredients. Cover and simmer for 15 minutes or until broccoli is tender.

Onion Cheese Casserole

8 servings

Here's a contest winner that's a rich, smooth, flavorful casserole. It puts homemade taste on your table without any fuss at all.

- 6 large onions, peeled and cut into ¼-inch wedges
- ¾ cup water
- 3 cups (12 ounces) shredded Cheddar cheese
- 1 cup all-purpose flour
- 1 cup chopped scallions
- ½ cup plus ¼ cup grated Parmesan cheese
- 1 garlic clove, minced
- ¼ cup fresh bread crumbs

Place onions and water in a large saucepan. Cover and simmer for 20 to 30 minutes, stirring occasionally, or until onions are tender; drain. Preheat oven to 350°F. In a large bowl, combine the cooked onions, Cheddar cheese, flour, scallions, the ½ cup Parmesan cheese, and garlic. Place onion mixture in a greased 2-quart casserole. In a small bowl, mix together the remaining ¼ cup Parmesan cheese and bread crumbs; sprinkle over onion mixture. Bake for 35 minutes or until top turns golden brown.

NOTE: This is a great side dish for meat, chicken, or fish—whatever you like!

Easy Corn Fritters

about 24 fritters

Great for breakfast, lunch, snacks, or whatever–and always with that down-home taste you'll remember.

- 1 cup all-purpose flour
- 1 cup canned cream-style corn (one 7- to 8-ounce can)
- 1 cup canned whole kernel corn, drained (one 7- to 8-ounce can)
- ½ cup milk
- 1 egg, well beaten
- 1 teaspoon baking powder
- 1 teaspoon vegetable oil
- ½ teaspoon salt
- ⅛ teaspoon pepper
- Butter or margarine for frying

In a large bowl, combine all ingredients, except butter; mix well. In a large skillet, melt butter; drop batter by tablespoonsful onto hot skillet. When bubbles appear, turn and brown on other side. Serve hot.

NOTE: So many toppings go great with fritters–sugar, jam, syrup, applesauce, or cranberry sauce. Serve these with your favorites.

Health Salad

about 8 servings

Most of the time, when we hear the word "health" in a recipe title we chuckle and wonder just how good it could really be, right? But sometimes we're really surprised at the wonderful taste of certain food combinations. Try this surprise!

- 1 small head purple cabbage, shredded (about 8 cups)
- 3 or 4 apples, peeled, cored, and finely chopped
- ½ cup golden raisins
- ½ cup apple juice
- ½ cup mayonnaise
- 1 tablespoon dried dillweed or 2 tablespoons chopped fresh dill

In a large bowl, combine all ingredients. Let stand in refrigerator for at least 2 hours to "marry" the flavors. (Overnight is best!) Store in refrigerator until ready to serve.

NOTE: Serve with a sandwich for lunch or as a dinner "go-along." This will keep in the refrigerator for up to 3 days.

Country Coleslaw

about 10 servings

Good old-fashioned coleslaw. It's right any time of year with any kind of meal. This is the creamy mayonnaise kind that we loved as kids.

- 1 cup mayonnaise
- 3 tablespoons fresh lemon juice
- 2 tablespoons sugar
- 1 teaspoon salt
- 6 cups shredded cabbage (a small head of cabbage yields about 8 cups)
- 1 cup shredded carrots (about 3 carrots)
- ½ cup chopped or thinly sliced green bell pepper

In a large bowl, combine mayonnaise, lemon juice, sugar, and salt. Add cabbage, carrots, and green pepper; toss to coat well. Cover; chill.

NOTE: This may be stored in the refrigerator for up to 3 days.

Herbed Vegetable Medley

6 servings

This is a salad that's a bit more exotic and creative, and oh yes, very easy to prepare.

- 1 can (14 ounces) artichoke hearts, drained and halved
- 2 medium-sized tomatoes, cut into wedges
- 1 green bell pepper, cut into chunks
- 1 cup fresh mushrooms, halved or quartered
- 1 cup sliced celery
- 1 cup pitted ripe olives, drained

MARINADE

- ⅔ cup white vinegar
- ⅔ cup olive or vegetable oil
- ¼ cup chopped onion
- 2 garlic cloves, minced
- 2 teaspoons sugar
- 1 teaspoon dried basil, crushed
- 1 teaspoon dried oregano, crushed
- 1 teaspoon salt
- ¼ teaspoon black pepper

In a large saucepan, combine all marinade ingredients; simmer, uncovered, for 10 minutes. In a large bowl, combine the remaining ingredients. Add the warm marinade to the vegetable mixture and stir to coat vegetables. Cover; chill for several hours or overnight, stirring occasionally. Drain before serving.

NOTE: This may be stored in the refrigerator for up to 2 days.

Sweet Onion Stir-Fry

4 to 6 servings

Oh, those sweet spring fresh crunchy "eat-'em-like-an-apple" onions!! What they can do in stir-fry!

- 2 large sweet onions
- 2 to 3 medium-sized zucchini
- 2 to 3 tablespoons peanut oil
- 1 tablespoon sesame seed
- Salt or soy sauce to taste
- Pepper to taste
- Garlic powder (optional)

Peel the onions and slice in half lengthwise; then slice into strips along the grain of the onion, forming strips about ½ inch wide. Wash zucchini and trim away ends. Cut each zucchini in half lengthwise, then cut crosswise into ½-inch slices. In a large skillet or wok, heat peanut oil; sauté onions, zucchini, and sesame seed over high heat, stirring frequently. Cook vegetables until just tender, remove from heat, and add salt and pepper and garlic powder, if desired. Serve immediately.

Sunday Night Corn Pudding

about 6 servings

H*ere's one of the easiest corn pudding recipes ever. There's really nothing to it but mixing. Is that easy enough??*

- 1 can (17 ounces) cream-style corn
- 1 can (17 ounces) whole kernel corn, drained
- ¼ cup milk
- 3 tablespoons sugar
- 2 eggs, beaten
- 2 tablespoons cornstarch

Preheat oven to 350°F. In a large bowl, mix together all ingredients. Pour mixture into a greased 2-quart casserole. Bake for 70 minutes, until firm and golden.

Belgian Sprouts

about 4 servings

I *know a lot of people don't like Brussels sprouts. But if you ever wanna change that opinion, this is the best way to do it. Magnificent! (They won't believe they're sprouts!)*

- 3 cups fresh Brussels sprouts (or two 10-ounce boxes frozen sprouts)
- 1/4 cup olive oil
- 1/2 large onion, chopped
- 1 teaspoon dried parsley flakes
- 1 teaspoon garlic powder
- 1/4 teaspoon salt
- 1/4 teaspoon pepper
- 1/2 cup chicken broth

Cook fresh Brussels sprouts until tender or thaw sprouts if frozen. In a large skillet, heat olive oil; brown sprouts in oil with onion, parsley flakes, garlic powder, salt, and pepper. Add chicken broth and cook until liquid reduces, about 3 to 4 minutes.

NOTE: You can substitute chunks of broccoli or cauliflower for the Brussels sprouts, if you prefer.

Stuffed Tomatoes

4 servings

These are old-fashioned tasty and new-fashioned easy! They really color up a plate, too.

- 4 large ripe tomatoes
- 4 tablespoons olive oil, divided in half
- 1 medium-sized onion, chopped
- 6 garlic cloves, minced
- 6 anchovies, chopped
- ¼ cup chopped fresh parsley
- ½ cup dry bread crumbs
- 2 tablespoons dry white wine
- ¼ teaspoon salt
- ¼ teaspoon pepper
- Grated Parmesan cheese for sprinkling (optional)

Preheat oven to 350°F. Cut tops off tomatoes; remove the center pulp; set tomato shells aside. Chop the center pulp and set aside, discarding excess juice. In a large skillet, heat 2 tablespoons olive oil; add onion and garlic and sauté just until softened. Add tomato pulp, anchovies, parsley, bread crumbs, wine, remaining olive oil, salt, and pepper; mix well. Fill tomato shells with mixture and place in a greased 8-inch square baking dish. Sprinkle with Parmesan cheese, if desired. Bake for 20 minutes or until cheese is melted and lightly golden.

Chopped Broccoli Casserole

4 servings

This is a hearty dish that's either a great go-along or a meal in itself.

- 1 package (10 ounces) frozen chopped broccoli, thawed
- ½ can (5 ounces) cream of mushroom soup
- ½ cup (2 ounces) grated Cheddar cheese
- ½ cup mayonnaise
- 1 egg
- 1 teaspoon finely chopped onion
- ⅛ teaspoon cayenne pepper (optional)
- ½ cup crumbled cheese snack crackers
- 1 tablespoon butter, melted

Preheat oven to 350°F. Squeeze excess water from thawed broccoli and drain well. Place broccoli in a large bowl; mix in mushroom soup, grated cheese, mayonnaise, egg, onion, and cayenne pepper, if desired. Pour mixture into a 1-quart casserole that has been coated with nonstick vegetable spray. Mix crumbled crackers with melted butter, then sprinkle evenly over top of casserole. Bake for 30 to 35 minutes, until bubbly.

NOTE: You can use chopped asparagus instead of broccoli. Whatever you prefer!

Stewed Zucchini and Tomatoes

4 to 6 servings

This has a wonderful flavor that goes with any meal, and the best part is it'll even make your kitchen smell like Mama's!

- 3 tablespoons vegetable oil
- 3 garlic cloves, finely chopped
- 1 medium-sized onion, coarsely chopped
- 3 tomatoes, seeded and coarsely chopped
- 3 medium-sized zucchini, sliced into rounds
- 1½ to 2 teaspoons salt
- ½ teaspoon pepper
- 1 teaspoon dried oregano
- 1 teaspoon dried basil

In a large saucepan, heat oil; sauté the garlic and onion until tender. Add the tomatoes and continue cooking until tomatoes soften, about 5 to 10 minutes. Add the remaining ingredients and cook for 15 to 20 minutes more or until zucchini is soft. Serve immediately.

NOTE: This is so easy; it tastes even fresher with fresh basil and parsley if you have them handy!

Every Mama's Favorite Cucumber Salad

about 8 cups

Have a lot of extra fresh cucumbers? Here's a great go-along for any meal. Mama used to throw it together in a jiffy. We can, too.

- 8 cups thinly sliced cucumbers (about 5 cucumbers)
- 1 large onion, thinly sliced
- 1½ cups white vinegar
- ½ cup sugar
- 3 garlic cloves, finely chopped (or 1½ teaspoons bottled chopped garlic)
- 1 tablespoon vegetable oil
- 4 teaspoons salt
- 1 cup water
- ½ teaspoon white pepper
- 3 tablespoons chopped fresh dill (or 1 to 2 tablespoons dried dillweed)

In a large bowl, combine cucumbers and onion; set aside. In a large saucepan, mix together the vinegar, sugar, garlic, oil, salt, and water; bring to a boil, stirring frequently. Pour mixture over the cucumbers and onion; add the pepper and dill and mix well. Keep refrigerated. Serve well chilled.

NOTE: This may be stored in the refrigerator for up to 4 days.

California Casserole

10 to 12 servings

This seems so California trendy (even though it's from "way back when")!

- 4 jars (6 ounces each) marinated artichoke hearts, drained
- 3 packages (10 ounces each) frozen chopped spinach, thawed and drained
- 2 packages (8 ounces each) cream cheese, softened
- ¾ cup milk
- 5 tablespoons butter, softened
- ½ cup grated Parmesan cheese

Preheat oven to 350°F. Grease a 9″ × 13″ baking dish. Cut up artichoke hearts and arrange in the bottom of the baking dish. Spread spinach on top. In a large bowl, mix together the cream cheese, milk, and butter; dollop cream cheese mixture on top of spinach, then spread carefully with a knife. Sprinkle Parmesan cheese over top. Bake for 30 to 40 minutes or until heated through.

NOTE: If you need to save time, prepare this dish a day ahead, cover, and refrigerate. Before you're ready to serve, bake casserole in a preheated oven and serve hot.

Fresh Throw-Together Salad

4 to 6 servings

This is just mixing together and couldn't be easier! Keep some on hand in the fridge for crunchy snacking.

- 1 bunch broccoli, cut into florets
- 1 head cauliflower, cut into florets
- 1 bunch scallions, chopped
- 1 cup mayonnaise (or to desired moistness)
- ½ cup grated Parmesan cheese
- Salt to taste
- Pepper to taste

In a large bowl, mix together all ingredients and stir to coat broccoli and cauliflower florets. Serve cold, so keep refrigerated. It will keep for up to 2 days.

Breads and Muffins

We're not about to devote the time Mama did to making breads and muffins, not very often, anyway. But we *can* capture those same tastes and textures a lot easier today. We have shortcuts, better equipment, and super mixes that give us lots of help.

A basket of homemade muffins or a rich, moist cake-type bread can make an entire meal taste and feel homemade (even if the rest of the meal is full of our shortcuts). Whether a snack, go-along, or a touch of sweet for dessert, all of these treats can say, "Welcome to our house," "Thank you," or "We fussed a bit 'cause you're special." Yet, they're all so easy!

Wait 'til you see these that were so popular on my TV show. Now, when they're done they don't look or taste easy, so you're guaranteed to find some favorites that you'll make over and over again. Won't blame ya!!

Mighty Muffins

6 muffins

Sometimes one special item on the table will make the whole meal seem special–like these big, big muffins. Not only are they a snap to make, but they'll also make a great conversation piece!

- 1¼ cups all-purpose flour
- 1 cup cornmeal
- ⅓ cup sugar
- 1½ teaspoons baking powder
- ½ teaspoon baking soda
- ¼ cup buttermilk powder
- 1 cup (4 ounces) shredded sharp Cheddar cheese
- 1 cup water
- 1 egg
- 4 tablespoons (½ stick) butter or margarine, melted
- 1 can (4 ounces) mild chilies, chopped

Preheat oven to 375°F. In a large bowl, mix flour, cornmeal, sugar, baking powder, baking soda, and buttermilk powder. Reserve 2 tablespoons Cheddar cheese; stir remaining cheese into flour mixture and set aside. In a small bowl, blend water, egg, melted butter, and chopped chilies; add to flour mixture. Stir just until lightly blended (batter will be lumpy). Grease 6 6-ounce custard cups; spoon batter equally into custard cups. Top with reserved cheese. Place cups on a cookie sheet or in a shallow baking pan, allowing room between them, and bake for 35 to 40 minutes or until tops are golden. Let cool for about 5 minutes, then remove from cups and serve warm.

NOTE: If buttermilk powder is not available, use 1 cup buttermilk and *omit* the water. Muffin pans will work here also but, depending on the size you use, your yield will vary. Custard cups really work the best.

Chocolate Zucchini Bread

2 loaves

H*ow many times have you wondered what to do with all the zucchini around? Well, here's a "chocolaty" answer to that question! Yes, chocolate. Don't laugh! And boy, does it startle them when you tell them!*

- 3 cups all-purpose flour
- 2 cups sugar
- 1 teaspoon baking soda
- 1 teaspoon ground cinnamon
- ½ teaspoon salt
- ¼ teaspoon baking powder
- ¼ cup baking cocoa
- 3 eggs, beaten
- 2 cups grated zucchini (about 1 large)
- 1 cup vegetable oil
- 1 cup chopped pecans
- 1 teaspoon vanilla extract

Preheat oven to 325°F. In a large bowl, mix together the flour, sugar, baking soda, cinnamon, salt, baking powder, and cocoa. In another bowl, combine remaining ingredients. Stir zucchini mixture into flour mixture. Grease well and lightly flour two 9″ × 5″ loaf pans; divide mixture evenly between the loaf pans. Bake for 1 hour or until wooden toothpick inserted in center comes out clean. Cool for 10 minutes on a rack, then remove from pan. Cool completely before slicing.

Quick Bread

1 loaf

Quick, yes, but packed with all the old-fashioned flavor you'll love. Now, it's not a regular-type bread. It's more like a "cakey" bread, so slice it thick and smear it with your favorite spread, such as cream cheese, honey, jam, whatever. Mmmm . . . you can almost smell it baking!

- 2 cups all-purpose flour
- 2 tablespoons sugar
- 2 teaspoons baking powder
- 3/4 teaspoon dried sage, crushed
- 1/4 teaspoon baking soda
- 1/4 teaspoon salt
- 2 eggs
- 1 cup buttermilk
- 3 tablespoons olive oil
- 1/2 cup (2 ounces) shredded Cheddar cheese
- 1/2 cup medium pitted ripe olives, drained and sliced

Preheat oven to 350°F. In a large bowl, mix together the flour, sugar, baking powder, sage, baking soda, and salt. In another bowl, combine the eggs, buttermilk, and olive oil; beat to mix well. Add egg mixture to flour mixture, stirring just until moistened; fold in the cheese and olives. Pour batter into a greased 9″ × 5″ loaf pan. Bake for about 45 minutes or until a wooden toothpick inserted near the center comes out clean. Cool in pan for 10 minutes; remove from pan and cool on wire rack. Wrap and chill overnight before slicing.

Fresh Apple Cinnamon Muffins

12 muffins

These become a secret ingredient that goes into that basket on the table and makes it a "you-made-it-yourself" meal. And they're so easy.

- 1½ cups all-purpose flour
- ⅓ cup granulated sugar
- 2 teaspoons baking powder
- 1 teaspoon ground cinnamon, divided
- ½ teaspoon salt
- 1 egg
- ½ cup milk
- 1 cup finely chopped apple (about 1 large, peeled and cored)
- 4 tablespoons (½ stick) butter, melted
- ⅓ cup chopped nuts (any kind)
- ¼ cup firmly packed brown sugar

Preheat oven to 375°F. In a large bowl, combine the flour, granulated sugar, baking powder, ½ teaspoon of the cinnamon, and salt. In another bowl, beat the egg with milk, then stir in the apple and melted butter; add all at once to flour mixture and stir until just moistened (batter will be very stiff). Spoon batter into a greased muffin tin(s), filling each cup about ⅔ full. In a small bowl, combine nuts, brown sugar, and remaining ½ teaspoon cinnamon; sprinkle mixture over muffin tops. Bake for 15 to 20 minutes or until wooden toothpick inserted in center of a muffin comes out clean. Remove from pan immediately and serve warm.

Banana Date Bread

1 loaf

E*ven though we call it a bread this can be more of a dessert. And topped with cream cheese or butter it's even better!*

- ¼ cup vegetable oil
- ½ cup sugar
- 1 egg, beaten
- 1½ cups all-purpose flour
- 2 teaspoons baking powder
- ½ teaspoon baking soda
- ½ teaspoon salt
- 1½ cups mashed ripe banana (3 to 4 bananas)
- 2 tablespoons water
- 1 teaspoon vanilla extract
- 1 cup chopped pitted dates (1 10-ounce container is about 1½ cups)
- ½ cup chopped nuts

Preheat oven to 350°F. In a large bowl, beat together the oil and sugar. Add the egg and mix well. In a medium-sized bowl, combine the flour, baking powder, baking soda, and salt. In another bowl, combine the banana, water, and vanilla extract. Add banana mixture to the oil-and-sugar mixture alternately with the flour mixture, mixing well after each addition. Stir in the dates and nuts. Turn mixture into a greased and floured 9″ × 5″ loaf pan. Bake for 50 to 55 minutes or until a wooden toothpick inserted in the center of the loaf comes out clean. Cool for 10 minutes, then remove from pan and let cool on wire rack before slicing.

Holiday Quick Bread

1 loaf

This is one of those cake-textured breads that can be changed so easily to fit the bill for every season. One recipe, but all seasons. Nice! Nice!

BASIC BATTER

- 1 cup sugar
- 4 tablespoons vegetable oil
- 1 cup milk
- 1 egg
- 1 teaspoon vanilla extract
- 2 cups all-purpose flour
- 3 teaspoons baking powder
- 1 teaspoon salt

Preheat oven to 350°F. In a large bowl, mix together the sugar, oil, milk, egg, and vanilla extract; beat well. Add the flour, baking powder, and salt. Pour batter into a greased and floured 9″ × 5″ loaf pan. Bake for 50 to 60 minutes or until a wooden toothpick inserted in center of the loaf comes out clean. Cool for 10 minutes, then remove from pan and let cool on wire rack; serve.

To Make Cranberry Bread: Add 1 teaspoon orange extract, 1 teaspoon ground cinnamon, and 1½ cups chopped cranberries to Basic Batter. Bake as above.

To Make Fresh Apple Bread: Use ingredients as above, except divide sugar, and mix together ¾ cup sugar (of the 1 cup total), vegetable oil, milk, egg, and vanilla extract in a large bowl; beat well. Add flour, baking powder, and salt. Pour half the batter into a greased and floured 9″ × 5″ loaf pan. Toss 2 cups cored, peeled, and chopped apples with the remaining ¼ cup sugar and place apples over batter in loaf pan. Pour remaining batter over apples. Bake as above.

Cheese Bread

6 to 8 servings

Got the gang coming over at the last minute? OK, throw some burgers on the grill and make this bread for your everything else, your everything easy. It's so novel compared to everybody else's regulars.

- 1 loaf French bread
- ½ cup (1 stick) butter or margarine, softened
- 1 teaspoon dried dillweed
- 1 cup (4 ounces) grated Cheddar or mozzarella cheese
- 1 garlic clove, crushed, or ½ teaspoon bottled garlic

Slice bread in half lengthwise. In a bowl, combine remaining ingredients and spread on one half of the loaf. Put the bread halves together and wrap in aluminum foil. While cooking your main course, warm on grill (away from the coals) for about 20 minutes or until cheese melts. Slice and serve immediately.

NOTE: For a change, serve grilled hamburgers or chicken breasts on this instead of buns. You can even start with garlic bread and simply add the dill and cheese. To make indoors, heat in a 350°F. oven for about 20 minutes or just until the cheese melts. This can even make a great appetizer!

Holiday Corn Bread

12 servings

The main reason everybody made corn bread years ago was that it was so easy to throw together. Well, it still is, and we can turn that same easy into holiday-fancy if we want!

- 1 cup all-purpose flour
- 1 cup cornmeal
- ½ cup sugar
- ½ cup shredded coconut
- ½ cup finely chopped nuts
- ⅓ cup (5⅓ tablespoons) butter or margarine, softened
- 1 tablespoon baking powder
- ½ teaspoon salt
- ½ teaspoon ground cinnamon
- ½ teaspoon ground nutmeg
- ¾ cup milk
- 1 egg yolk

Preheat oven to 500°F. In a large bowl, combine the flour, cornmeal, sugar, coconut, nuts, butter, baking powder, salt, cinnamon, and nutmeg; mix until it's the consistency of sand. In a small bowl, combine the milk and egg yolk. Make a well in the middle of the cornmeal mixture and add the milk–egg yolk mixture; stir until completely moist. Pour into a greased 8-inch square baking dish. Bake for 15 to 20 minutes or until golden brown and a wooden toothpick inserted in the center of the loaf comes out clean. Cool slightly, then cut into serving-sized pieces.

Blueberry Muffins

16 muffins

Wanna see your family's eyes light up? Wouldn't ya just love to put a basket of blueberry muffins on the Sunday breakfast table? Well, you can–and with no fuss!

- 2½ cups plus 2 tablespoons all-purpose flour
- 2½ teaspoons baking powder
- ¼ teaspoon salt
- 1 cup sugar, divided, plus extra for sprinkling
- 1 cup milk
- 2 eggs, beaten
- ½ cup (1 stick) butter or margarine, melted
- 1½ cups fresh blueberries, washed

Preheat oven to 400°F. In a large bowl, mix the 2½ cups flour, baking powder, salt, and ¾ cup of the sugar. Add the milk, eggs, and butter and mix only until dry ingredients are dampened. Mix the berries with the 2 tablespoons flour and ¼ cup sugar. Fold berries into batter. Spoon batter into greased muffin tins, filling two-thirds full. Sprinkle with sugar and bake for 20 to 25 minutes or until golden and a wooden toothpick inserted in the center of a muffin comes out clean.

Texas Corn Bread

12 to 15 servings

Here's a prize-winning recipe that nobody can ignore and everybody loves. It's not the typical corn bread. It's a pudding-textured corn bread that we use as a side dish 'cause it's so moist and rich. Sure is novel!!

- 1½ cups self-rising cornmeal
- 4 eggs, beaten
- ¾ teaspoon salt
- 1 cup chopped green bell pepper
- 1 cup (4 ounces) grated Cheddar cheese
- 1 cup chopped onion
- 3 tablespoons sugar
- 1 teaspoon baking powder
- 1 cup sour cream
- 1 can (17 ounces) cream-style corn
- ½ cup vegetable oil

Preheat oven to 450°F. In a large bowl, mix together all ingredients. Pour mixture into a 9″ × 13″ baking dish that has been coated with nonstick vegetable spray and bake for 20 to 30 minutes or until a wooden toothpick inserted in the center comes out clean. Remove from oven and cut into serving-sized squares.

NOTE: If self-rising cornmeal is not available, use a mixture of ¾ cup flour, ¾ cup cornmeal, 1 teaspoon salt, and 1 tablespoon baking powder; it will make 1½ cups self-rising cornmeal. The original recipe calls for a stick of butter to be melted and poured evenly over the warm bread before serving. If that sounds good to you, why not give it a try?!

Date Nut Bread

1 loaf

W*hen you have a homemade rich and chewy date nut bread on hand in the fridge or freezer, you can be an instant hero. It's what Mama would make when she wanted to treat us.*

- 2 cups chopped pitted dates
- ⅔ cup firmly packed brown sugar
- ½ cup honey
- 2 tablespoons butter or margarine
- 1 cup very hot water
- 1 egg, beaten
- 2 teaspoons vanilla extract
- 2 cups all-purpose flour
- 1 teaspoon baking soda
- ½ teaspoon salt
- 1 cup chopped walnuts

In a large bowl, combine dates, sugar, honey, and butter. Add hot water, stir; let stand for 15 minutes. Preheat oven to 325°F. Stir egg and vanilla into date mixture. In a separate bowl, combine remaining ingredients. Stir the flour mixture into the date mixture. Pour batter into a greased 9″ × 5″ loaf pan and bake for 1 hour or until a wooden toothpick inserted in the center of the loaf comes out clean. Cool in the pan for 10 minutes, then remove from pan and allow to cool completely on a wire rack.

NOTE: This bread is great with breakfast, lunch, brunch, or in your dinner roll basket. And it's even easier if you buy the dates already chopped!

"Quickie" Garlic Bread

4 to 6 servings

Garlic bread is right almost anytime. I like this one 'cause it's plain and simple–and tasty!–and great served with fruit and wine.

- 1 cup (4 ounces) shredded Cheddar cheese
- 1 cup grated Parmesan cheese
- 1 cup mayonnaise
- ½ teaspoon garlic powder
- 1 loaf Italian or French bread, split lengthwise

Preheat oven to broil. In a large bowl, combine cheeses, mayonnaise, and garlic powder. Spread mixture on bread and broil for a few minutes, until cheese top is golden brown and bubbly. Slice and serve immediately.

NOTE: Sometimes I get more creative and sprinkle it with some basil, rosemary, or chili powder. Or you can top it with sliced tomatoes, then add a drizzling of a bottled pesto sauce, then a sprinkle of cheese and broil it as above. Mmm . . . Mmm!!

Hawaiian Pineapple Banana Bread

2 loaves

Bring a little Hawaii to your table! What a great combination of pineapple, banana, and nuts. Serve it with your favorite spread and you'll be the kitchen whiz of the neighborhood.

- 3 cups all-purpose flour
- 2 cups sugar
- 1 teaspoon baking soda
- 1 teaspoon ground cinnamon
- ¾ teaspoon salt
- 1 cup chopped pecans or walnuts
- 3 eggs, beaten
- 1 cup vegetable oil
- 2 cups mashed ripe bananas (about 5)
- 2 teaspoons vanilla extract
- 1 can (8 ounces) crushed pineapple, drained

Preheat oven to 350°F. In a large bowl, combine the flour, sugar, baking soda, cinnamon, and salt; stir in pecans. In a separate bowl, combine remaining ingredients; mix well. Pour wet mixture into dry mixture, stirring just until dry ingredients are moistened. Spoon batter into 2 greased and floured 8″ × 4″ loaf pans. Bake for about 1½ hours or until a wooden toothpick inserted in the center of a loaf comes out clean. Cool in pans for 10 minutes; remove from pans and let cool on wire racks.

NOTE: In Hawaii they'd use macadamia nuts, but pecans or walnuts are more affordable and work just as well.

Cranberry Muffins

12 to 15 muffins
(depending on size of muffin cups)

There's no better way to set a homestyle table than with homemade muffins, and cranberries are truly Americana. Here's Mama, homemade, and Americana all in one.

- 2 cups all-purpose flour
- ¼ cup plus 1 tablespoon sugar
- 2 teaspoons baking powder
- ½ teaspoon salt
- ¾ cup milk
- ½ cup (1 stick) butter or margarine, melted
- 1 egg, beaten
- 1 cup canned whole-berry cranberry sauce (a 16-ounce can contains about 1½ cups)

Preheat oven to 400°F. In a large bowl, combine the flour, the ¼ cup sugar, baking powder, and salt; mix well. In a separate bowl, combine the milk, butter, and egg; mix well. Stir the liquid mixture into the dry mixture just until moistened. Fold in the cranberry sauce. Fill greased muffin cups two-thirds full with batter. Sprinkle tops with the remaining 1 tablespoon sugar and bake for about 25 minutes or until golden brown and a wooden toothpick inserted in the center of a muffin comes out clean.

NOTE: When they're in season, try chopping fresh cranberries (instead of canned) into the batter, but be sure to add some extra sugar to make up for their natural tartness. Serve these muffins plain or with cream cheese, jam, or a topping.

Desserts

Why take time introducing this chapter? There's no need 'cause everybody knows what sweet pangs of ecstasy we get when we envision our favorite desserts, whether they're gooey, full of custard or whipped cream, or rich and laden with fruit and nuts.

From cookies to ice cream pies or smooth cheesecakes, the recipes that follow are all quick as can be, simpler than ever. Some may sound difficult, but they're much easier than Mama's all-day-at-the-stove versions . . . with the same great tastes. Why, some don't take any cooking at all, they're just mixing!

Regardless of the rest of the meal, dessert is what they'll remember 'cause that's what they had last. Desserts can make us the star of the dinner crowd, or any crowd.

Sure, we're more weight-conscious lately. But a small piece of a great dessert can sometimes be just the treat we need for our usual carefulness the rest of the time. You know what you can and can't have. Find something and make it your own. And if you want Mama's tastes (but lots easier), they're here! (Guess I couldn't resist saying something about desserts, after all!)

Fruit Cocktail Cake

6 to 9 servings

Remember when you were a kid and the big prize in your fruit cocktail was an extra grape or the red cherry? Well, it's the same with this throw-together cake.

- 2 cups all-purpose flour
- 1½ cups sugar
- 2 teaspoons baking powder
- ¼ teaspoon salt
- 2 eggs
- 1 teaspoon vanilla extract
- 2 cups fruit cocktail with juice
- Whipped topping for garnish

Preheat oven to 350°F. In a large bowl, combine the flour, sugar, baking powder, and salt; set aside. Place the eggs in another bowl; beat well, then add the vanilla extract and fruit cocktail. Fold the fruit mixture into the dry ingredients and mix well. Pour batter into a greased 9-inch square baking pan. Bake for 40 minutes or until a wooden toothpick inserted in the center comes out clean. When cool, cover with whipped topping.

Soda-Fountain Special

6 to 8 servings

W*e can bring back the past with this soda-fountain pie! It's something the kids'll love to eat, and they'll want to help make it, too!*

- 1 prepared 9-inch graham cracker pie crust
- 2 medium-sized firm bananas, sliced
- 1 pint each vanilla, chocolate, and strawberry ice cream, slightly softened
- Chocolate, butterscotch, and strawberry ice cream toppings
- 1 container (8 ounces) frozen whipped topping, thawed
- 1 tablespoon chopped nuts
- Maraschino cherries (optional)

Line bottom and sides of the pie shell with banana slices. Place small scoops of each flavor of ice cream over banana slices, alternating flavors to create a design. Drizzle with ice cream toppings. Freeze pie for 1 hour. Before serving, top with whipped topping and nuts. Garnish individual slices with cherries, if desired.

NOTE: If freezing overnight, dip banana slices in lemon juice so they won't turn brown. Use your favorite flavors and the desired amount of ice cream and toppings to create your own soda-fountain smorgasbord.

Raisin Nut Pie

6 to 8 servings

This nutty "rich and chewy" reminds me of autumn, but it's great any time of the year.

- 3 eggs, lightly beaten
- ¾ cup dark corn syrup
- ½ cup firmly packed light brown sugar
- ¼ cup (½ stick) butter or margarine, melted
- 1 teaspoon vanilla extract
- ¼ teaspoon salt
- 1 cup raisins
- ½ cup chopped pecans or walnuts
- 1 unbaked 9-inch pie shell

Preheat oven to 350°F. Place the eggs in a large bowl and beat in corn syrup, brown sugar, butter, vanilla extract, and salt until well blended. Stir in raisins and nuts; pour mixture into the pie shell. Bake for 40 to 50 minutes or until a knife inserted in the center of the pie comes out clean. Cool and serve.

NOTE: If you prefer, you can make your own pie shell, but a store-bought one works fine.

Pineapple Pudding

4 to 6 servings

When you need a lift, put together this simple pudding that'll remind you of a tropical island.

- 1 can (20 ounces) crushed pineapple, undrained
- 3 eggs, well beaten
- ½ cup sugar
- 2 tablespoons all-purpose flour
- 1 teaspoon salt
- 4 slices white bread, cubed
- ½ cup (1 stick) butter or margarine, melted

Preheat oven to 350°F. In a large bowl, combine the undrained pineapple and eggs. In another bowl, mix together the sugar, flour, and salt; add to pineapple mixture. Pour batter into a greased 1½-quart baking dish. Toss bread cubes in the melted butter; place over pineapple mixture. Bake for 45 to 50 minutes or until lightly golden.

NOTE: Serve warm or cold and garnish with a dollop of plain whipped topping or with whipped topping that has a little cherry pie filling added to it.

Dump Cake

10 to 15 servings

The '50s are still popular for lots of reasons, including the foods that we loved. This recipe will bring you back. And when they ask you about the name, you'll have fun explaining the "dump" part! And it's quick and easy, too!

- 1 can (21 ounces) cherry pie filling
- 1 small can (8 ounces) crushed pineapple, undrained
- 1 box (18.25 ounces) yellow cake mix
- 1 cup chopped pecans
- 1 stick (½ cup) butter, cut into pieces

Preheat oven to 350°F. Grease a 9" × 13" baking pan. Dump in the pie filling and smooth it evenly over the bottom of the pan. Next dump in the undrained pineapple and smooth. *Do not mix.* Dump in the dry cake mix, then the nuts, again smoothing, not mixing, after each addition. Place the butter pieces on top and bake for 1 hour or until lightly golden.

NOTE: Serve with ice cream, if you like. You can also try different things every time you make it–like different fruit pie fillings, white cake mix, or walnuts or almonds.

Strawberries Romanoff

6 to 8 servings

There's nothing easier or fancier than fresh strawberries. Enjoy these with a little Russian twist of orange!

- 1 quart fresh strawberries (about 4 cups)
- 3 tablespoons sugar
- ¼ cup fresh orange juice
- 1 teaspoon orange extract
- Whipped cream for garnish

Wash and hull berries; gently pat dry. Leave berries whole or slice as desired, and place in a large bowl; sprinkle sugar lightly over the berries. In a small bowl, mix the orange juice with the orange extract and pour over the sweetened berries. Cover and refrigerate until well chilled. Spoon berries and syrup into individual glasses and garnish with whipped cream.

Strawberries Romanoff Cake

6 to 8 servings

Here's that Russian twist of orange with strawberries in a smooth cake. What a simple way to rival the fancies!

- 1 plain pound cake
- ¾ cup strawberry preserves
- ½ teaspoon orange extract
- 2 cups frozen whipped topping, thawed (an 8-ounce container is 3½ cups)

Split the pound cake in half lengthwise. In a large bowl, mix the remaining ingredients together. Place about half the strawberry mixture between the 2 layers of pound cake, then cover the cake with the remaining mixture. Serve immediately or chill until ready to serve.

NOTE: If you like, you can garnish the cake with fresh strawberries. If you really feel like splurging, you can use homemade sponge cake, real whipped cream, and other types of berries (depending on the season).

Easy Lemon Mousse

4 to 6 servings

I*f you're looking for a cool and refreshing dessert, this is it. It's a snap, too!*

- 1½ cups heavy cream
- ⅓ cup sugar
- ¼ cup freshly squeezed lemon juice
- 1 teaspoon lemon extract
- Fresh grated lemon peel for garnish (optional)

In a large bowl, beat together all ingredients, except garnish, until mixture starts to mound softly. Spoon into dessert dishes and serve, garnished with grated lemon peel, if desired.

NOTE: For a nice change, try freshly squeezed lime juice and lime extract instead of lemon. Topped with berries, it's a lemon- or lime-berry mousse. Serve with plain cake and it's a mousse cake. You get the picture!

Fudgy Brownies

about 30 servings

No matter how many goodies we make, one of the top favorites is still brownies. These taste like the fudge brownies we remember as kids!

- 2 sticks (8 ounces) butter or margarine, melted
- ¾ cup baking cocoa
- 2 cups sugar
- 4 eggs
- 1 cup all-purpose flour
- 2 teaspoons vanilla extract
- ½ teaspoon salt
- 1 package (12 ounces) semisweet chocolate chunks
- 1 cup chopped nuts (optional)

Preheat oven to 350°F. Place melted butter into a large bowl; add cocoa and stir until well blended. Add sugar; mix well. Add eggs, one at a time, beating well after each addition. Add flour, vanilla extract, and salt; stir *just until mixed together.* Stir in chocolate chunks and nuts. Spread batter in a greased 9″ × 13″ baking pan; bake for about 30 minutes or until done. Cool and cut into serving-sized pieces.

NOTE: Semisweet chocolate chips may be substituted for chunks.

Two-Tone Holiday Pie

6 to 8 servings

You don't have to make a mincemeat pie and *a pumpkin pie. Here's the way to serve both of everybody's favorite pies in one!*

- ¾ cup mincemeat (canned or bottled)
- 1 prepared 9-inch graham cracker pie crust
- 1 egg, slightly beaten
- 1 cup canned pumpkin
- ¼ cup orange juice
- ½ cup evaporated milk
- ½ cup sugar
- ¼ teaspoon salt
- ¾ teaspoon ground cinnamon
- Dash of ground ginger

Preheat oven to 350°F. Spread the mincemeat over the bottom of the pie crust. In a large bowl, combine remaining ingredients. Pour mixture over mincemeat and bake for 50 to 60 minutes or until golden. Cool fully before serving.

NOTE: Serve cooled pie with a dollop of whipped cream or whipped topping. You can use a prepared pie shell or make your own, whatever you prefer.

"T.L.B.S." (Tastes Like Banana Split)

10 to 12 servings

If you want to keep a winning treat ready in the refrigerator, here's an easy "make-ahead" dessert.

- 2 cups graham cracker crumbs
- 6 tablespoons butter or margarine, melted
- 2 packages (3.5 ounces each) instant vanilla pudding and pie filling
- 3 bananas, sliced
- 1 can (20 ounces) crushed pineapple in heavy syrup, drained
- 1 container (12 ounces) frozen whipped topping, thawed
- Ground nuts for garnish
- Maraschino cherries for garnish

In a medium-sized bowl, mix together the graham cracker crumbs and butter; pat mixture into a 9″ × 13″ baking dish and set aside. In a large bowl, prepare the pudding according to package directions. Spread pudding evenly over graham cracker crumbs; cover with banana slices, then pineapple and whipped topping. Keep refrigerated; garnish with nuts and cherries just before serving.

NOTE: This is best served firm, so, if possible, refrigerate overnight.

Pumpkin Squares

35 squares

Great for a party, a holiday, or any time you want to have a rich, moist, tasty dessert on hand. Even though pumpkin reminds you of autumn, today it's enjoyable year 'round. (In fact, a dessert like this can be a bigger hit out of season.)

- 2 cups all-purpose flour
- ½ teaspoon salt
- 1 teaspoon baking powder
- 1 teaspoon baking soda
- 1 teaspoon ground cinnamon
- 1 teaspoon nutmeg
- 4 eggs
- 1 can (16 ounces) pumpkin
- 1½ cups sugar
- 1 cup vegetable oil
- 1 teaspoon vanilla extract

Preheat oven to 350°F. In a large bowl, sift or mix together well the flour, salt, baking powder, baking soda, cinnamon, and nutmeg. In another large bowl, beat together the eggs, pumpkin, sugar, oil, and vanilla extract. Gradually add the flour mixture to the pumpkin mixture; beat well. Pour batter into a 9″ × 13″ baking dish that has been coated with nonstick vegetable spray. Bake for 30 minutes or until a wooden toothpick inserted in the center comes out clean. Let cool in pan on a wire rack.

NOTE: Cool completely before covering with whipped topping or your favorite frosting.

Pumpkin Pie Pudding

8 servings

W*hen fall rolls around, I really get in the mood for pumpkin everything. Well, here's another way to enjoy that good old-fashioned pumpkin pie flavor, but it's easier and faster than pie.*

- 1 can (30 ounces) pumpkin pie filling
- 1 teaspoon ground cinnamon
- ½ teaspoon nutmeg
- 1 container (8 ounces) frozen whipped topping, thawed

In a large bowl, mix pie filling, cinnamon, and nutmeg. Fold whipped topping into pumpkin mixture just enough to create a marbled effect. Spoon mixture into custard cups or fancy glasses. Refrigerate until ready to serve.

Impossible Pumpkin Pie

6 to 8 servings

F*unny name for a pie. I guess it got this name because it's so* impossibly *delicious and* impossibly *easy! No crust to make because it forms its own crust. Hooray!!*

- 1 can (16 ounces) pumpkin
- 1 can (12 ounces) evaporated milk
- 2 tablespoons butter or margarine, softened
- 2 eggs
- ¾ cup sugar
- ½ cup biscuit baking mix
- 2½ teaspoons pumpkin pie spice
- 2 teaspoons vanilla extract

Preheat oven to 350°F. Place all ingredients in a blender jar and blend on high for 1 minute or place all ingredients in a large bowl and beat for 2 minutes with a hand beater. Pour mixture into a greased 9- or 10-inch pie plate. Bake for 50 to 60 minutes or until knife inserted in center comes out clean. Cool before serving.

White on White Cake

18 to 24 servings

Here's a cake that's as good for snacking as it is for serving at a holiday dinner. Thanks to my friend Ethma for this one. She remembered it from way back.

- 1 box (18.25 ounces) white cake mix
- 1 can (15 ounces) cream of coconut
- 1 container (8 ounces) frozen whipped topping, thawed
- 1 package (12 to 14 ounces) frozen fresh coconut or 1 package (14 ounces) flaked coconut

In a 9″ × 13″ baking pan, bake cake according to package directions. Using a fork, prick holes in baked cake; spoon cream of coconut over it. Cool completely. Spread whipped topping over the cake, then sprinkle on *all* the coconut. Refrigerate any leftover cake.

NOTE: For a special holiday treat, decorate the cake with your own colorful toppings. Cream of coconut is used in tropical drinks as well as in cooking and baking.

Tapioca Pudding

4 servings

Remember when Mama used to make tapioca? It was one of the standards years ago. Well, it's still a popular family favorite, but now it's fast and easy to make.

- 2½ tablespoons small pearl tapioca
- 1 large egg, slightly beaten
- 2½ tablespoons sugar
- ⅛ teaspoon salt
- 1¾ cups milk
- ½ teaspoon vanilla extract

Place the tapioca in a small bowl; add just enough cold water to cover the tapioca pearls. Let soak for 30 minutes; drain. In a saucepan, combine the tapioca, egg, sugar, salt, and milk. Cook over medium heat, stirring frequently, until pudding boils and is thick enough to coat a spoon. (The pudding will thicken further as it cools.) Remove from heat and let stand for 15 minutes, stirring occasionally. Add vanilla extract; mix well. Pour into a large bowl or 4 individual serving dishes and refrigerate until ready to serve.

Glow Tarts

6 servings

Here's a "throw-together" treat that fits not only now, but any time you want an easy way to say, "I made it just for you." And what these do to a holiday buffet table!!

- ½ cup sugar
- ¼ cup (½ stick) butter or margarine, melted
- 2 eggs
- 5 teaspoons all-purpose flour
- 5 teaspoons fresh lemon juice
- 1 package (6 shells) graham cracker tart shells
- 1 golden delicious apple, peeled, cored, and cut into ⅛-inch rings (about 6 slices)

APPLE GLAZE

- 3 tablespoons apple jelly
- 1 tablespoon fresh lemon juice

Preheat oven to 350°F. In a medium-sized bowl, combine the sugar and margarine; mix well. Add the eggs, one at a time, beating well after each addition. Add the flour and the 5 teaspoons lemon juice; mix well. Spoon mixture into tart shells; top each tart with an apple slice. Place tarts on a cookie sheet and bake for 20 minutes or until set. Allow tarts to cool. Meanwhile, combine apple glaze ingredients in a small saucepan; stir over low heat until jelly melts. Top cooled tarts with glaze and refrigerate until ready to serve.

Peach Cookie Sundae

8 servings

This sounds like it's right out of Mama's stay-at-home-all-day cookbook, but there's really nothing to it!

- 1/4 cup sugar
- 4 tablespoons cornstarch
- 1/2 teaspoon ground cinnamon
- 1/4 cup light corn syrup
- 5 cups peaches, peeled and sliced (about 2 1/2 pounds)
- 1 package (20 ounces) refrigerator chocolate chip cookie dough, cut into 1/4-inch slices

Preheat oven to 350°F. In a large bowl, stir together the sugar, cornstarch, cinnamon, and corn syrup. Add the peaches; mix well. Pour mixture into a greased 8-inch square baking dish and top with cookie dough slices. Bake for about 30 to 40 minutes or until golden brown. Cool before serving.

NOTE: You don't have to peel the peaches if you don't want to—it'll look even more like Mama's old-fashioned best! (This is great topped with ice cream, too!)

Best Cookie Ever

about 5 dozen cookies

If you feel like bragging, bake these cookies for the gang. You'll be able to say, "I baked the best cookies ever"! That's what they'll be saying, too.

- ½ pound (2 sticks) butter, softened (not margarine)
- 1 cup granulated sugar
- 1 cup firmly packed brown sugar
- 2 eggs
- 1 teaspoon vanilla extract
- 2 cups all-purpose flour
- 2½ cups rolled oats
- 1 teaspoon baking soda
- 1 teaspoon baking powder
- ½ teaspoon salt
- 1 bag (12 ounces) chocolate chips
- 1 plain semisweet or milk chocolate bar (8 ounces), grated
- 1½ cups chopped nuts (such as almonds, walnuts, or pecans)

Preheat oven to 375°F. In a large bowl, cream together the butter and sugars. Mix in the eggs and vanilla extract. Mix in the flour, oats, baking soda, baking powder, and salt. Add the remaining ingredients and mix together. Roll dough into small balls (no larger than Ping-Pong ball size) and place about 2 inches apart on lightly greased cookie sheets. Bake for 6 to 7 minutes.

NOTE: To be sure that the cookies are moist and chewy, don't overbake.

Easiest Cheesecake Ever

6 to 8 servings

Everybody loves cheesecake, and you'll especially love this one because you don't have to bake it. It's a little different, too—more like an ice cream cheesecake pie.

- 1 small package (3 ounces) cream cheese, softened
- 2 tablespoons sugar
- ½ cup milk
- 1 cup finely crushed toffee candy (reserve 2 tablespoons for garnish)
- 1 container (8 ounces) frozen whipped topping, thawed
- 1 prepared 9-inch graham cracker pie crust

In a large bowl, combine the cream cheese, sugar, and milk using a hand mixer. Mix in the crushed candy, then fold in the whipped topping. Spoon mixture into the pie crust; freeze for about 4 hours. Sprinkle reserved candy on top of cheesecake before serving.

NOTE: If toffee candy is not available, use finely crushed toffee candy bars, like Heath® or Skor® candy bars.

Chocolate Chocolate Chip Cake

6 to 10 servings

E*verybody loves chocolate,* and *everybody loves chocolate chips. Well, here they are together, a winning combination that'll make* you *a winner!*

- 1 box (18.25 ounces) devil's food chocolate cake mix
- 1 large package (5.25 ounces) instant chocolate pudding and pie filling
- 1 cup sour cream
- 1 cup vegetable oil
- 4 eggs, beaten
- ½ cup warm water
- 1 package (12 ounces) semisweet chocolate chips or morsels

Preheat oven to 350°F. In a large bowl, mix together the cake and pudding mixes, sour cream, oil, eggs, and water. Stir in the chocolate chips and pour batter into a well-greased 12-cup Bundt pan. Bake for 50 to 55 minutes or until top is springy to the touch and a wooden toothpick inserted in the center comes out clean. *(Do not overbake.)* Cool cake thoroughly in pan; invert and remove from pan.

NOTE: Serve plain, sprinkled with confectioners' sugar, drizzled with warm icing, or with vanilla or coffee ice cream.

Cookie Pie

6 to 8 servings

Just put out the word that you're gonna make a cookie pie—that's right, a chocolate chip cookie in a butter-flavored crust—and they'll come running!

- 2 eggs
- ⅓ cup all-purpose flour
- ⅓ cup granulated sugar
- ⅓ cup firmly packed brown sugar
- 1 stick (½ cup) butter or margarine, melted and cooled to room temperature
- 1 small package (6 ounces) semisweet chocolate chips or morsels
- ⅔ cup chopped walnuts
- 1 prepared 9-inch butter-flavored pie crust

Preheat oven to 325°F. In a large bowl, beat the eggs with a mixer until foamy. Add the flour and sugars, beating until blended. Blend in butter. Add chocolate chips and walnuts and mix. Pour mixture into pie crust and bake for 1 hour or until golden brown.

NOTE: You can use your own homemade pie crust, if you prefer.

Microwave Brownie/Cake/Cupcake Mix

7 cups

H*ere's an all-in-one brownie/cake/cupcake mix that doesn't involve heating up the kitchen, 'cause we use the microwave. Isn't that easy? And with your own mix . . . it's always handy.*

- 3 cups sugar
- 2 cups all-purpose flour
- 2 cups baking cocoa
- 1½ teaspoons baking powder

Combine all ingredients in a large resealable plastic bag (or a large bowl); seal bag. Shake or mix until ingredients are thoroughly combined. Store mix in plastic bag or in a tightly covered container. Shake or mix well before using in microwave brownie, cake, or cupcake recipes.

Microwave Brownies

12 to 18 brownies

- 2 cups Microwave Brownie Mix (page 251)
- 2 eggs
- ½ cup mayonnaise

In a large bowl, combine all ingredients; stir until well blended. Spread mixture evenly in a 10″ × 6″ microwaveable baking dish that has been coated with nonstick vegetable spray. Microwave at medium (50%) for 6 minutes, turning once. Turn dish again and microwave at high (100%) for 3 minutes longer or until surface is firm to the touch. Cool.

Microwave Chocolate Cake

about 8 servings

- 2 cups Microwave Brownie Mix (page 251)
- 2 eggs
- ½ cup mayonnaise
- ½ cup milk
- Frosting (optional)

In a large bowl, combine the brownie mix, eggs, mayonnaise, and milk; stir until well blended. Pour mixture into a 9″ round microwaveable cake dish that has been coated with nonstick vegetable spray. Microwave at medium (50%) for 7 minutes, turning once. Turn dish; microwave at high (100%) for 3 minutes longer or until a wooden toothpick inserted 1 inch from edge comes out clean. Cool in dish. Frost, if desired.

Microwave Chocolate Cupcakes

6 cupcakes

1 cup Microwave Brownie Mix (page 251)
1 egg
¼ cup mayonnaise
¼ cup milk
Frosting (optional)

Line 6 microwaveable muffin pan cups with paper liners. In a medium-sized bowl, combine the brownie mix, egg, mayonnaise, and milk; stir until well blended. Spoon mixture into muffin cups. Microwave at high (100%) for 3 minutes, turning once. Cupcakes will appear moist; let cool. Frost, if desired.

NOTE: To make without microwaveable muffin pan: Use 2 paper liners for each cupcake. Arrange in circular pattern on microwaveable plate. Proceed as above. Cupcakes will spread slightly.

Please note that cooking time for each recipe is based on full power (600- to 700-watt) microwave ovens.

Mint Cream Pie

6 to 8 servings

H*ere's just the ticket when you're looking for something green* and *delicious for St. Patrick's Day. But it's not just for the holiday; your leprechauns will be asking for it all year long!*

- 6 cups miniature marshmallows
- ¼ cup milk
- ⅓ cup green *crème de menthe*
- 1 teaspoon vanilla extract
- 3 or 4 drops green food color
- 1 container (8 ounces) frozen whipped topping, thawed, or whipped cream
- 1 prepared chocolate-flavored 9-inch pie crust

In a saucepan, combine the marshmallows and milk; cook over low heat, stirring, until marshmallows melt. Remove from heat; cool, stirring every few minutes until partially set. Stir in the liqueur, vanilla extract, and food color; fold in whipped topping and pour into pie crust. Freeze until firm. Before serving, let stand for 10 minutes.

NOTE: Garnish with grated chocolate, if you like.

Apple Spice Custard Cake

12 to 15 servings

Looking for something new and *easy to do with apples? Here's a cake that's tangy and sweet at the same time. And it tastes so down-home apple-chunky that nobody even dreams that it starts with a mix!*

- 1 box (18.25 ounces) spice cake mix
- 2 medium-sized apples, peeled, cored, and finely chopped (about 2 cups)
- 1 can (14 ounces) sweetened condensed milk
- 1 cup sour cream, at room temperature
- 1/4 cup lemon juice
- Ground cinnamon for garnish

Preheat oven to 350°F. Prepare cake mix according to package directions; stir in apples. Pour batter into a well-greased and floured 9″ × 13″ baking dish. Bake for 30 minutes or until a wooden toothpick inserted in center comes out clean. Meanwhile, in a medium-sized bowl, combine sweetened condensed milk, sour cream, and lemon juice. After cake is removed from oven, spread milk-sour cream mixture over top. Return cake to oven and bake for 10 minutes more or until set, like custard. Sprinkle with cinnamon. Cool completely. Store in refrigerator.

Yam Banana Pudding

6 to 8 servings

Years ago, we only had banana pudding when Mama didn't want a couple of overripe bananas to go to waste. Today it's still a favorite, and we can make it whether we have overripe bananas or not!

- 1 cup mashed banana (ripe is best)
- 2 cups peeled, cooked, and mashed sweet potatoes (2 to 3 large or about 1 17-ounce can)
- ½ cup milk
- ½ cup sour cream
- ½ cup orange juice
- ⅓ cup firmly packed light brown sugar
- ¼ cup (½ stick) butter or margarine, melted
- 1 tablespoon grated orange rind
- ½ teaspoon pumpkin pie spice
- ¼ teaspoon salt
- 4 eggs, separated

Preheat oven to 350°F. In a large bowl, combine all ingredients, except egg whites. In a separate bowl, beat egg whites until stiff; fold them into banana mixture. Pour mixture into a greased 2-quart baking dish. Bake for 1¼ hours or until golden.

NOTE: Serve hot or cold with whipped cream or whipped topping, if you'd like.

New Sweet Potato Pie

16 servings

Nothing is more down-home Americana than sweet potato pie. Think it's hard to make? Not this one! It's so easy. And do they ever rave (and beg for the recipe, too)! It's like a candy pie–yup, that good!!

- 1 package (8 ounces) cream cheese, softened
- 2 eggs, beaten
- ¾ cup sugar
- 2 prepared 9-inch graham cracker pie crusts
- 2 packages (3½ ounces each) instant vanilla pudding and pie filling
- ¾ cup milk
- 2 cups peeled, cooked, and mashed sweet potatoes, (2 to 3 large or about 1 17-ounce can)
- Dash of ground cinnamon
- 1½ cups frozen whipped topping, thawed, divided (an 8-ounce container is 3½ cups)
- ½ cup chopped nuts (optional)

Preheat oven to 350°F. In a medium-sized bowl, mix together well the cream cheese and eggs. Add the sugar and beat until fluffy. Spread mixture into pie crusts and bake for 20 minutes; let cool. Meanwhile, in a large bowl, stir together the pudding mix and milk until smooth and thick. Add the sweet potatoes and cinnamon and mix well; fold in 1 cup whipped topping. Spread sweet-potato mixture on cooled pies. Garnish with remaining ½ cup whipped topping and sprinkle with chopped nuts. Store in refrigerator.

Brownie Sin

8 to 10 servings

Here's a special dessert that doesn't take a lot of work. I bet the kids'll help make it. I know they'll help eat it! (The name helps the eating and the eating helps the name!)

- 1 box (21 to 24 ounces) fudge brownie mix
- 1 can (14 ounces) sweetened condensed milk
- ½ cup cold water
- 1 box (3½ ounces) instant vanilla pudding and pie filling
- 1¾ cups frozen whipped topping, thawed (an 8-ounce container is 3½ cups)
- About 1 quart fresh strawberries, cleaned, hulled, and halved

Preheat oven to 350°F. Grease two 9-inch round layer cake pans. Line with wax paper, extending up sides of pans; grease wax paper. Prepare brownie mix according to package directions for cake-like brownies, then pour mixture into prepared pans. Bake for 20 to 25 minutes or until top springs back when touched; cool. Meanwhile, mix sweetened condensed milk and water in a large bowl; beat in pudding mix. Chill for 5 minutes. Fold in whipped topping. Place 1 brownie layer on a serving plate. Top with half the pudding mixture, then half the strawberries. Add second brownie layer, then remaining pudding mixture and strawberries. Keep refrigerated.

NOTE: You can use frozen berries instead of fresh or chocolate cake mix instead of brownie mix.

Apples in Syrup

4 to 8 servings

Used up all your apple tricks and still want to try something different? Know how everybody loves the sticky syrup you get when you make baked apples? It's here! Mmm . . . Mmm!

- 6 to 8 red cooking apples, peeled or unpeeled
- 4 tablespoons (½ stick) butter or margarine
- ¼ cup sugar
- ¼ cup apple juice or cider
- ¼ teaspoon ground cinnamon

Core the apples and cut them into thin wedges. In a large skillet, heat butter over low heat; add apples, sugar, apple juice, and cinnamon. Cover; simmer for 15 to 20 minutes. Uncover and continue cooking for 5 to 10 minutes more or until apples are glazed and tender, stirring occasionally.

NOTE: This is great served with whipped cream or whipped topping. Remember that the cooking time may vary slightly depending on the type of apple you use.

Cherry Sour Cream Tortes

8 servings

D*elicious, quick,* and *easy–everything we could ever want in a dessert! And there's no cooking! Do you realize how fast these can be thrown together?*

- 24 chocolate cookie wafers
- 1 container (16 ounces) sour cream
- 1 can (21 ounces) cherry pie filling and topping

In each of 8 individual serving dishes, layer 1 chocolate cookie wafer, a generous tablespoon of sour cream, and 1 tablespoon cherry pie filling. Repeat with two more layers. Chill for about 1 hour before serving.

Impossible Cheese Pie

8 to 10 servings

Impossible¿¿ Never!! Easy¿¿ Always!! And the taste and texture are like cheesecake is supposed to be.

- 3 eggs
- 1 cup sugar
- 1 teaspoon vanilla extract
- 2 packages (8 ounces each) cream cheese, softened
- 1 container (16 ounces) sour cream
- ⅓ cup biscuit baking mix

Preheat oven to 350°F. Place all ingredients in a blender jar and blend until no streaks remain. Pour batter into a greased 10-inch deep dish pie plate. Bake for 30 to 35 minutes. Turn off oven and allow pie to remain in oven for 1 hour before removing. Chill.

NOTE: Serve plain or with your favorite fresh berries or other fruit topping.

Two-Minute Hawaiian Pie

6 to 8 servings

Want to stay out of the kitchen at holiday time or when friends drop over? If you have two minutes, just two, you can, and you'll have a dessert to serve that everybody'll love.

- 1 large package (5.25 ounces) instant vanilla pudding and pie filling
- 1 can (20 ounces) crushed pineapple in syrup, undrained
- 1 container (8 ounces) sour cream
- 1 prepared 9-inch butter-flavored pie crust
- Sliced pineapple for garnish
- Maraschino cherries for garnish
- ½ cup flaked coconut for garnish

In a large bowl, combine the vanilla pudding mix, undrained crushed pineapple, and sour cream; mix until well blended. Pour mixture into pie crust. Decorate with sliced pineapple and cherries and sprinkle with coconut. Chill for at least 2 hours before serving.

NOTE: Don't make the vanilla pudding according to package directions; just add the dry instant pudding mix to the other ingredients.

Wacky Cake

9 to 12 servings

Wacky cake–that's right–wacky! It's an old-time cake that's always a little bit different, but always a pleaser and a conversation starter.

- 1½ cups all-purpose flour
- 1 cup sugar
- ⅓ cup baking cocoa
- 1 teaspoon baking soda
- ½ teaspoon salt
- 1 teaspoon vanilla extract
- 2 teaspoons white vinegar
- ⅔ cup vegetable oil
- 1 cup water

Preheat oven to 350°F. Mix together the flour, sugar, cocoa, baking soda, and salt; place in an ungreased 8-inch square baking pan. Make 3 wells in the mixture. Pour vanilla extract into the first well, vinegar into the second, and oil into the third. Pour the water over the entire mixture; mix well. Bake for 30 to 40 minutes or until a wooden toothpick inserted in the center comes out clean.

NOTE: If you'd like to use a 9″ × 13″ baking pan, double the amounts of all the ingredients. You can garnish the cooled cake slices with a dollop or two of Whipped Chocolate Frosting (page 264). And it's "wacky," because it often falls a bit in the center.

Whipped Chocolate Frosting

enough for an 8 × 8-inch cake

This is one of my favorite frostings because, like Wacky Cake (page 263), it's a little different. Why not try them together?

- 1 package (about 3.5 ounces) instant chocolate pudding and pie filling
- 1 cup milk
- 3 cups frozen whipped topping, thawed (an 8-ounce container is 3½ cups)

In a large bowl, mix the instant pudding and milk with an electric beater on low for 1 minute. Add the whipped topping and mix thoroughly with beater.

Irish Potato Candy

30 to 36 balls

Years ago, around St. Patrick's Day, a lot of mothers would make this sweet, fresh treat. This recipe is simple, yet just as timely as way back when. Oh, yes, one more thing–there are no potatoes in it!

- ¼ cup (½ stick) butter or margarine, softened
- 4 ounces cream cheese, softened
- 1 teaspoon vanilla extract
- 1 box (16 ounces) confectioners' sugar
- 1 bag (7 ounces) flaked coconut (about 2½ cups)
- Ground cinnamon for rolling

In a large bowl, cream together the butter and cream cheese. Beat in the vanilla and confectioners' sugar, then mix in the coconut. Roll mixture between hands to form walnut-sized balls. Roll balls in cinnamon and refrigerate until firm.

NOTE: Use good-quality, regular cream cheese, not whipped or light varieties.

Tres Leches

12 to 15 servings

This sure isn't a diet cake, but when you want that special treat this is it! The name means "three milks," and it's a favorite Hispanic dessert that's becoming very popular throughout the country. There's almost no work and no cooking involved at all here, 'cause this is the shortcut method.

- 1 can (14 ounces) sweetened condensed milk
- 1 can (12 ounces) evaporated milk
- 1 pint half-and-half
- Pinch of salt
- 2 pound cakes (12 ounces each)
- 1 container (8 ounces) frozen whipped topping, thawed

In a large bowl, combine the sweetened condensed milk, evaporated milk, half-and-half, and salt; stir well and set aside. Cut the pound cakes into 6 slices each. Lay slices tightly in the bottom of a 9″ × 13″ baking dish. Pour milk mixture evenly over the cake slices, cover, and refrigerate for about 2 to 3 hours. Remove from refrigerator and spread whipped topping over cake. Chill for an additional 1 to 2 hours. (There will still be some liquid on the bottom of the pan because this is more like a pudding than a regular cake and should be eaten with a spoon.)

NOTE: It's fine to make your own pound cakes, but store-bought ones really do the job. It's traditional to eat this plain, but go ahead and garnish with fresh berries, other fresh fruit, or your favorite pie filling before serving, if you want.

Summer Ambrosia

4 servings

This isn't a true ambrosia but, like Mama, we can use whatever is available to whip up a special one. Yes, Mama had the knack and so can we when we create a cool and delicious summer treat with in-season items. Nothing's easier!

- 2 cups sliced peaches
- ½ cup blueberries, cleaned
- 1 banana, sliced
- 1 tablespoon fresh lime or lemon juice
- ⅓ cup flaked coconut

In a large bowl, lightly toss together the peaches, blueberries, banana slices, and lime juice. Transfer to serving bowl and chill for at least 30 minutes. Sprinkle with coconut just before serving.

NOTE: For an even more "summery" ambrosia, I sometimes add some nectarines, plums, or mangoes.

Genets

36 cookies

Remember those wonderful Italian cookies made for special occasions like weddings or holidays? They're delicious, and they make any day special. Thanks, Lana!

- 5 cups all-purpose flour
- 1 cup granulated sugar
- 5 teaspoons baking powder
- 1 cup vegetable oil
- 1 cup milk
- Pinch of salt
- 2 teaspoons fresh lemon juice
- 2 eggs

FROSTING

- 3 cups sifted confectioners' sugar
- 4 tablespoons (½ stick) butter or margarine, melted
- 6 tablespoons orange juice
- 2 teaspoons fresh lemon juice
- 2½ teaspoons vanilla extract

Rainbow sprinkles for topping

Preheat oven to 350°F. In a large bowl, mix together the flour, sugar, baking powder, oil, milk, salt, 2 teaspoons lemon juice, and eggs. Roll dough into balls (to make 36) and place on cookie sheets coated with nonstick vegetable spray. Bake for about 15 minutes, until set but not brown. Meanwhile, in another large bowl, mix together the frosting ingredients until mixture is smooth and all lumps are gone. Dip tops of cooled cookie balls in frosting, then sprinkle with rainbow sprinkles.

Zabaglione Tarts with Fresh Berries

6 servings

Need a dessert in a hurry? Here's a delicious Italian-style treat that can be made at the last minute and left in the refrigerator while you're having dinner. Now that's what I call easy!

- 1 cup milk
- 2 tablespoons Marsala wine
- 1 package (about 3.5 ounces) instant vanilla pudding and pie filling
- ½ cup frozen whipped topping, thawed (an 8-ounce container is 3½ cups)
- 1 package (6 shells) graham cracker tart shells
- 18 medium-sized fresh strawberries, hulled and halved

In a blender jar, place the milk, wine, and pudding mix; cover and blend on low until well mixed and slightly thickened. Remove to a bowl and fold in whipped topping. Divide filling among 6 tart shells and arrange strawberries on top. Chill until ready to serve.

NOTE: Top with additional whipped topping, if desired. You can also use raspberries or blueberries instead of the strawberries.

Cannoli Filling

filling for 8 cannoli shells

W*hat's a more classic Italian pastry than cannolis? Thought you could only get them in an old-fashioned Italian bakery? Guess again. Now you can make them right in your own kitchen!*

- ¾ cup confectioners' sugar
- 1 container (15 ounces) ricotta cheese
- 1 teaspoon vanilla extract
- ½ cup miniature chocolate chips
- Dash of ground cinnamon (optional)
- 8 cannoli shells

In a large bowl, blend the sugar with the ricotta cheese. Add the vanilla, then mix in the chocolate chips and cinnamon until evenly distributed. Fill cannoli shells, dividing mixture evenly among shells.

NOTE: Cannoli shells are usually available at the supermarket, or they can be found in Italian import stores.

Depression Cake

2 loaves (16 servings)

One of the things the Depression of the 1930s did was to make everybody very creative in the kitchen, but with inexpensive ingredients. My Mama made a simple cake that was so tasty we kept asking for it years later. It still doesn't cost that much to make, but the taste is richer than ever.

- 1 box (15 ounces) raisins (2½ cups)
- 3 cups water
- 2 cups sugar
- 1 tablespoon butter or margarine
- 2 tablespoons ground cinnamon
- 1 teaspoon allspice
- 3½ cups all-purpose flour
- 1 heaping tablespoon baking soda

Preheat oven to 325°F. In a large saucepan or Dutch oven, combine the raisins, water, sugar, butter, cinnamon, and allspice; bring to a boil. Cook for 2 to 3 minutes, then set aside to cool. When cool, stir in the flour and baking soda. (If mixture seems too thick compared to regular cake batter, add a little more water, a teaspoon at a time.) Grease and flour two 8″ × 4″ loaf pans; divide batter evenly between the pans. Bake for 60 to 70 minutes or until a wooden toothpick inserted in center comes out clean. Cool for 10 minutes, then remove from pan and let cool completely on a wire rack before slicing.

Holiday Honey Cake

12 to 15 servings

It tastes like Mama's—spicy, smooth, and moist. It will bring back memories of when we were kids. The big thing to remember here is DON'T OVERBAKE IT! Then you'll be sure to get a nice moist cake, the way it's supposed to be.

- 1 cup firmly packed brown sugar
- 1 cup honey
- ½ cup vegetable oil
- 4 eggs, beaten
- 3¼ cups all-purpose flour
- 1½ teaspoons baking powder
- 1 teaspoon baking soda
- ½ teaspoon ground cinnamon
- ½ teaspoon allspice
- ¼ teaspoon ground cloves
- 1 cup black coffee
- ⅓ cup plus ¼ cup raisins

Preheat oven to 350°F. In a large bowl, mix together well the brown sugar, honey, oil, and eggs. Add the flour, baking powder, baking soda, cinnamon, allspice, and cloves; mix well. Stir in coffee and the ⅓ cup raisins. Pour batter into a well-greased and lightly floured 12-cup Bundt pan. Sprinkle remaining ¼ cup raisins on top of batter and gently swirl into batter. Bake for 35 to 45 minutes or until a wooden toothpick inserted in center comes out clean. *Do not overbake.* Cool in pan on wire rack. After about 15 minutes, loosen edges with a table knife. Invert cake on rack and let cool completely.

NOTE: We reserve the ¼ cup raisins and swirl them in just before baking so they'll stay in the center of the cake instead of sinking to the bottom.

Easy Coffee Cake

10 to 16 servings

This cake smacks of Southern hospitality–no matter where you are! You'll feel good serving this to family and company. Every family had their favorite one, but it was never this easy. Thanks, Sema . . . love ya!

- 1 box (18.25 ounces) yellow cake mix
- 1 container (8 ounces) sour cream
- ¾ cup vegetable oil
- ½ cup granulated sugar
- 4 eggs
- 3 tablespoons firmly packed brown sugar
- 2 tablespoons ground cinnamon
- 1 cup chopped pecans

Preheat oven to 350°F. In a large bowl, mix together the cake mix, sour cream, oil, granulated sugar, and eggs. In a separate bowl, combine the remaining ingredients to make the filling/topping. Pour half the batter, about 2 cups, into a well-greased and lightly floured 12-cup Bundt pan. Sprinkle with half of the filling/topping, about 1 cup. Repeat the batter and filling/topping layers, then bake for about 1 hour or until a wooden toothpick inserted in the center comes out clean. Let cake cool on wire rack, then invert onto serving plate.

NOTE: Cake will probably fall after baking, but that's fine 'cause after it's inverted it won't matter! This is especially nice drizzled with a glaze made by mixing together 1 cup confectioners' sugar and 3 tablespoons milk. You can also try it with Cream Cheese Icing (page 274).

Cream Cheese Icing

Enough for one Bundt cake

E*ven though this goes with almost any cake, it's the perfect topping for Easy Coffee Cake* *(page 273)*.

- 1 small package (3 ounces) cream cheese, softened
- 2 tablespoons butter or margarine, softened
- 1 teaspoon fresh lemon juice
- 1 teaspoon milk
- Grated lemon rind
- 2 cups confectioners' sugar

In a bowl, mix together the cream cheese and butter until well blended. Beat in the lemon juice, milk, and grated lemon rind. Gradually beat in the confectioners' sugar until the mixture is of spreading consistency.

Rugelach

5 to 6 dozen

This recipe is of Eastern European origin (but the ice cream part is a new shortcut twist), and it'll give any kitchen that homey, irresistible aroma.

- 1 pound (4 sticks) butter, softened
- 4 cups all-purpose flour
- 1 pint vanilla ice cream, softened
- 1½ cups sugar
- ½ cup finely chopped nuts (any kind)
- ¼ cup ground cinnamon
- About ⅔ cup raspberry jelly
- About 1¼ cups raisins

In a large bowl, cut the butter into the flour. Add the softened ice cream and work it into the mixture with your hands. (Add more flour if necessary to make the dough easier to handle.) Cover and refrigerate dough overnight (it will become hard). The following day, preheat oven to 350°F. In a medium-sized bowl, combine the sugar, nuts, and cinnamon. Sprinkle about ⅕ of the sugar-nut mixture onto a clean pastry cloth, smooth dish towel, or smooth surface. Lightly flour a rolling pin; break off about ⅕ of the dough. Place dough on the sugar-nut mixture and roll it out (to about ⅛″ to ¼″ thickness) to form a circle. Spread about 2 tablespoons jelly and about ¼ cup raisins over rolled dough. Cut dough into small pie slice-shaped pieces (about 12 to 14 pieces) and roll up each piece from the outside to the center. Place rolls, seam-side down, on a cookie sheet that has been coated with nonstick vegetable spray. Repeat process, placing more sugar-nut mixture on your smooth surface each time before rolling out dough into circles, covering each dough circle with the jelly and raisins. Bake for about 30 minutes or until bottoms turn golden brown.

NOTE: You can leave out the raisins, if you prefer, but the flavor and texture are best with them.

Hodgepodge

Don't forget these! Here are those little items that I couldn't quite fit anywhere else. They fit into so many places and I use them so often that I want to be sure we can get to them fast!

So, definitely keep them in mind. They're the throw-together specials that elevate the ho-hum to something novel and exciting. Mama never hesitated, she always had something eyebrow-raising on the counter or table. Here are a few of the easy ones and wherever they fit is where you're sure to enjoy them.

Freezer Jam

What could be better than enjoying fresh berries year 'round? With Freezer Jam you can! Stock up on fresh extras when you can so you'll always have the heart-of-the-season taste at your fingertips. And you don't have to go through all the time, work, and mess of regular canning. Believe me, this is a lot easier.

Strawberry Freezer Jam

about 4½ cups

- 2 cups crushed fresh strawberries (about 4 cups sliced berries)
- 4 cups sugar
- 1 pouch (3 fluid ounces) liquid fruit pectin
- 2 tablespoons fresh lemon juice

In a large bowl, combine the strawberries and sugar; mix well. Let stand for 10 minutes. In a small bowl, combine the pectin and lemon juice; pour over strawberries. Stir thoroughly for 3 minutes (a few sugar crystals will remain). Spoon mixture into plastic containers; cover. Let stand at room temperature for 24 hours. Store in freezer.

Peach Freezer Jam

about 4 cups

- 2 cups pared, crushed fresh peaches (about 2 pounds)
- 3 1/4 cups sugar
- 1 pouch (3 fluid ounces) liquid pectin
- 3 tablespoons fresh lemon juice

In a large bowl, combine the peaches and sugar; mix well. Let stand for 10 minutes. In a small bowl, combine the pectin and lemon juice; pour over peaches. Stir thoroughly for 3 minutes (a few sugar crystals will remain). Spoon mixture into plastic containers; cover. Let stand at room temperature for 24 hours. Store in freezer.

Raspberry-Strawberry Freezer Jam

about 4 cups

- 1 cup crushed fresh raspberries (about 2 cups whole berries)
- 1 cup crushed fresh strawberries (about 2 cups whole berries)
- 4 cups sugar
- 1 pouch (3 fluid ounces) liquid fruit pectin
- 2 tablespoons fresh lemon juice

In a large bowl, combine the raspberries, strawberries, and sugar; mix well. Let stand for 10 minutes. In a small bowl, combine the pectin and lemon juice; pour over berries. Stir thoroughly for 3 minutes (a few sugar crystals will remain). Spoon mixture into plastic containers; cover. Let stand at room temperature for 24 hours. Store in freezer.

NOTE: Small amounts of jam can be stored in the refrigerator, covered, for 2 to 3 weeks.

Easy Cheese Soufflé

4 main-dish or 6 to 8 side-dish servings

I *know what you're thinking. A soufflé is too delicate, too touchy, too much of a pain in the neck to prepare. Well, not this one! Here's a sneaky way to make a cheese soufflé without all the work.*

- 4 eggs
- 3 cups milk
- Dash cayenne pepper
- ½ teaspoon dry mustard
- Salt to taste
- Black pepper to taste
- 6 white bread slices, crusts removed and slices cut in half diagonally
- 4 cups (16 ounces) grated Cheddar cheese

Preheat oven to 400°F. Grease a 2-quart soufflé or baking dish (with 4-inch sides). In a mixing bowl, thoroughly beat together the eggs, milk, cayenne pepper, dry mustard, salt, and black pepper. Line bottom of baking dish with 4 bread halves. Sprinkle with one-third of the cheese and pour one-third of the milk mixture on top; press down. Repeat layers twice. Press everything down lightly to saturate the bread. Bake for about 45 minutes or until brown and bubbly and knife inserted through the center shows that the bottom is set.

NOTE: For a creamier dish, prepare it ahead several hours or the morning before serving and refrigerate; then bake just before serving. (It may take 10 to 15 minutes longer to cook after being stored in the refrigerator.) You can also add 2 thickly sliced tomatoes, cooked broccoli, asparagus, green beans, or leftover ham or chicken to vary this dish a bit. Just add meat or vegetables on top of the bread-cheese-milk layers and press down. Repeat sequence twice, ending with meat or vegetables.

Horseradish French Dressing

2 cups

T*his dressing will enhance any salad. You'll see! And it couldn't be easier—or faster.*

- 1 cup ketchup
- ½ cup white vinegar
- ½ cup vegetable oil
- ¼ cup sugar
- 2 teaspoons salt
- 2 to 3 tablespoons horseradish
- 1 garlic clove, crushed

In a blender jar, combine all ingredients; blend until well mixed. Keep refrigerated.

Easy Cajun Seasoning Blend

⅓ cup

H*ow about having a little taste of excitement on the table to perk up the meal? It's as simple as seasoning!*

- 6 tablespoons vegetable oil
- 2 teaspoons dried thyme
- 1 teaspoon onion powder
- ¼ teaspoon salt
- ¼ teaspoon cayenne pepper

Combine all ingredients in a saucepan and stir over low heat for 1 minute. Use immediately or let cool and store in a tightly covered jar for up to 1 week.

NOTE: Brush on chicken, beef, seafood, veggies, or potatoes cooked on the grill or in the oven. Try adding a few teaspoons of this blend to gumbos or stews, too.

Melted Provolone in Tomato Sauce

4 servings

In the mood for a light meal but don't know what to fix? Want it to be something easy? No problem!

- 3 tablespoons olive oil
- 2 garlic cloves, minced
- 1 can (15 ounces) crushed tomatoes
- 1/4 teaspoon dried oregano
- 1/2 teaspoon dried basil
- Salt to taste
- Pepper to taste
- 1 pound (4 thick slices) Provolone cheese

In a large skillet, heat the olive oil until moderately hot; sauté the garlic for a few seconds. Add the tomatoes, oregano, basil, salt, and pepper. Reduce heat and simmer for about 15 minutes, stirring occasionally. Cut cheese slices in half and arrange over tomatoes; cover and cook over low heat until cheese begins to melt, about 4 minutes.

NOTE: Serve with a fresh garden salad and crisp Italian bread. Serve over pasta for a hearty meal. You can substitute Italian seasoning or thyme for the basil and you can save time by using bottled garlic instead of fresh. I also like to add a teaspoon of sugar for flavor variety.

Easy Caesar Dressing

about 4 cups

Who's got time to make Caesar Salad with today's busy schedules? You do, with this easy shortcut right at your fingertips in the fridge, and definitely keep it in the fridge.

- 2 cups olive or vegetable oil
- 1 tablespoon fresh lemon juice
- ½ cup red wine vinegar
- 4 garlic cloves, crushed
- 1 can (2 ounces) anchovies, drained
- 2 teaspoons prepared mustard
- 4 raw egg yolks
- 1 teaspoon Worcestershire sauce
- 1 cup grated Parmesan cheese
- 1 shake hot pepper sauce (optional)

In a blender jar, combine all ingredients and blend until smooth. As with any dish containing raw eggs, be sure to store dressing in the refrigerator until ready to use.

NOTE: I sometimes use a little more wine vinegar instead of adding the lemon juice and if I don't have anchovies on hand I substitute ½ can of chunk-style tuna and ¼ teaspoon salt for the anchovies. Everything works! This dressing is thick, so you can also use it as a veggie dip. If you have any concern over using a recipe containing raw eggs, then skip this one.

Blintz Soufflé

6 to 8 servings

A *meal in itself or a wonderful homey touch to any other meal. Boy, will this ever bring back memories of Mama and Sunday mornings!*

- 12 cheese blintzes (2 15-ounce boxes frozen blintzes, thawed)
- 6 eggs, beaten
- 1 container (16 ounces) sour cream
- ½ cup sugar
- 1½ teaspoons vanilla extract
- 2 tablespoons butter or margarine, melted

Preheat oven to 350°F. Coat a 9-inch square glass baking dish with nonstick vegetable spray. Lay blintzes out in baking dish and set aside. In a large bowl, beat together the eggs, sour cream, sugar, and vanilla extract. Pour mixture over blintzes, then drizzle melted butter over top. Bake for 1 hour, until golden.

Lemonade Base

about 2⅔ cups

There's nothing like a glass of homemade lemonade to quench thirst. Oh sure, it sounds like a lot of work, but it's easy–and delicious! With this base on hand, you'll just be adding water to get lemonade. Couldn't be easier. (And no more wasted lemons!)

- 1½ cups sugar
- ½ cup boiling water
- 1½ cups freshly squeezed lemon juice
- Grated peel of 1 lemon

Dissolve sugar in boiling water; remove from heat. Add lemon juice and peel. Let cool. Store lemonade base in covered container in the refrigerator or store in the freezer until needed. Just thaw, mix, and serve.

To Make Lemonade by the Glass: Combine ¼ cup lemonade base, ¾ cup cold water, and ice cubes.

To Make Lemonade by the Pitcher (about 8 cups): Combine 2⅔ cups lemonade base, 5 cups cold water, and ice cubes.

NOTE: Lemons will squeeze more easily at room temperature or if softened in the microwave (on low for a few seconds).

Sunshine Banana Smoothie

about 3 cups

Here's a clever way to use up those extra bananas that are starting to turn dark in the fruit bowl. Now they're turned back to delicious again!

1 peeled frozen banana, broken into chunks
4 to 5 fresh strawberries
1 cup orange juice
1 teaspoon creamy peanut butter (optional)

Combine all ingredients in a blender jar and blend until smooth.

NOTE: To freeze bananas, place peeled bananas on a cookie sheet, cover, and freeze or freeze in a plastic bag for about 2 hours. The frozen banana keeps the smoothie from being watered down, because it takes the place of ice. Peeled, frozen bananas keep for 2 weeks in the freezer. If you prefer a different taste, instead of strawberries and orange juice you can substitute your favorite fruits or juices with the frozen banana.

Italian Frittata

about 8 servings

Here's a great brunch idea. It'll look like you fussed but you'll know you didn't! This was always a ready-to-go snack in every Italian kitchen, and, boy, it never had the exact same things in it twice. Whatever was in the fridge went into the frittata.

- ¾ cup chopped onion
- ¾ cup chopped green bell pepper
- 8 eggs, beaten
- ¼ cup (1 ounce) grated Cheddar cheese
- ¼ teaspoon salt
- ¼ teaspoon black pepper
- ¼ teaspoon dried oregano
- ¼ teaspoon dried basil
- 1 to 2 tablespoons butter or margarine
- Grated Parmesan cheese (optional)

In a large bowl, mix together the onion, green pepper, eggs, Cheddar cheese, salt, black pepper, oregano, and basil. In a large nonstick skillet, melt butter; pour onion-green pepper mixture into hot skillet. Turn heat to medium-low, cover, and cook until mixture is solid, about 30 minutes. Turn out of skillet and cut into serving-sized portions. Sprinkle with Parmesan cheese before serving, if desired.

French Farmhouse Dressing

about 3½ cups

At the old French farmhouses the Mamas used to blend their dressings with a whisk, but today the blender makes it easier and less time-consuming. This is so much better than store-bought dressing, and so much less money, too.

- 1 can (10¾ ounces) tomato soup
- 1 cup vegetable oil
- ¾ cup cider vinegar
- ½ medium onion, grated
- ¼ cup sugar
- 1 garlic clove, crushed
- 1 tablespoon Dijon mustard
- 1 tablespoon horseradish (optional)
- 1 teaspoon Worcestershire sauce
- 1 teaspoon salt
- 1 teaspoon pepper

In a large bowl, combine all ingredients; mix well. (You can use a blender if you want, but it works just as well by hand.)

NOTE: Serve this sweet-and-sour dressing on your regular salad greens, spinach, or tomatoes—whatever.

Pancake Treats Italia

18 to 20 pancakes

These light little pancakes pack a whole lot of good–good tasting, good looking, good making. And they're perfect for dessert, brunch, or a special snack treat.

- 2 eggs
- 1 cup (8 ounces) ricotta cheese
- ½ cup all-purpose flour
- Grated peel of ½ lime
- Grated peel of ½ orange
- 2 tablespoons butter or margarine, melted
- ⅛ teaspoon salt
- ¼ teaspoon vanilla extract
- 2 teaspoons sugar
- Vegetable oil for frying

In a large mixing bowl, beat the eggs. Gradually stir in the ricotta cheese, then the flour. Combine the grated lime and orange peels, then blend them into the ricotta mixture with the remaining ingredients, except the oil. In a large skillet, heat the oil; drop the mixture by tablespoonsful into the hot oil. Brown pancakes on both sides, then drain on paper towels.

NOTE: These are really meant to be served with confectioners' sugar or warm honey.

Index

ABOUT THE AUTHOR

Art Ginsburg is best known as TV's lovable cooking celebrity, MR. FOOD®. His popular food news insert segment is the largest in the nation, seen in over 180 cities.

Twelve years ago Art became MR. FOOD® but long before that his life centered around food . . . and family. From running the family butcher shop to establishing the family catering business, Art has cultivated his many successes with his family by his side. Art's wife and three children all continue to work with him now in producing the MR. FOOD® television show, and his granddaughters appear to be Pop-Pop's three most enthusiastic fans.